"Even more than the God-given talents with which athletes are born, it is the heart and the spirit which provide the crucial difference between competitive feats and championship form. Gerald Harris' *Olympic Heroes: World Class Athletes Winning at Life* vividly demonstrates the faith which drives the Olympic athlete to excel. It should be an inspiration to us all."

NEWT GINGRICH
Speaker of the U.S. House of Representatives

"Gerald Harris' book, *Olympic Heroes,* will inspire and challenge you to be your best. The message of this book is timely, captivating, and sure to win the approval of its readers."

BOBBY BOWDEN
Head Coach, Florida State University
Seminole Football

"An enlightening, insightful, and absorbing book. *Olympic Heroes* is all about the art of living together as Christ taught. Gerald Harris has taken the field of sports and shown how it can inspire and motivate us all, while reminding us that the real path to glory goes through God's door."

NICK CHARLES
Sports Anchorman, CNN

"Dr. Harris inspires us with the lives of committed Olympic athletes who challenge us to fully develop the gifts God gives us while keeping our focus on Him."

STEVE DILS
Former NFL Quarterback

"Gerald Harris has reached into the gold mine of Olympic lore and extracted some fascinating stories. With insights and applications from the Bible, he has minted a book of inspiration of gold medal quality."

JIM HENRY
President of the Southern Baptist Convention and
Pastor of the First Baptist Church of Orlando, Florida

OLYMPIC HEROES

OLYMPIC HEROES

World-Class Athletes Winning At LIFE

Gerald Harris

Foreword By
Lenny Wilkens
Coach, 1996 US Olympic Basketball Team

Nashville, Tennessee

Published by
Broadman & Holman Publishers
Nashville, Tennessee

4262-91
0-8054-6291-0

Dewey Decimal Classification: 920.0
Subject Heading:
OLYMPIC GAMES / ATHLETES—BIOGRAPHY

Library of Congress Cataloging-in-Publication Data

Harris, J. Gerald, 1940- .
Olympic heroes : world class athletes winning at life / J. Gerald Harris.
p. cm.
ISBN 0-8054-6291-0 (pbk.)
1. Athletes—Biography. 2. Olympics—History. I. Title.
GV697.A1H348 1996
796'.092'2—dc20
[B] 95-48375
CIP

00 99 98 97 96 5 4 3 2 1

This book is dedicated to my parents, John and Shirley Harris, who have always been my greatest heroes, to my brother Truman whose athletic achievements always overshadowed mine, and to my sister Hope who is the greatest cheerleader two brothers could ever have.

CONTENTS

FOREWORD

Sporting events have attracted the attention of people all over the world. There's no greater sporting event than the Olympic Games. Olympic athletes have won the admiration of millions. Behind the extraordinary skill and athletic prowess of each Olympian, there are human interest stories to inspire and challenge all of us.

Most people cannot comprehend the time, the discipline, and commitment required to be a participant in the Olympic games. Some athletes have had to overcome almost insurmountable obstacles to qualify for the games. Others have had to overcome physical handicaps that have held most competitors back.

It would be interesting to observe the transformation that would occur in the whole of our society if the guiding principles of the Olympic athletes could be transferred to every segment of our culture. Excellence would become the norm; everyone would have a passion to succeed.

The essence of the Olympic Games promotes, not only excellence, but unity in the midst of diversity, camaraderie, and goodwill. When these virtues are governed and blessed by God's spirit, the results would be positive beyond our wildest imagination. In this book, you will find that the author has looked behind the scenes for insights into the greater meaning behind both the Olympics and life itself.

Lenny Wilkens
Coach, Atlanta Hawks
1996 U.S. Olympic Basketball Team

The Olympic Spirit

I lacked the quickness, the coordination, and the agility to succeed in basketball. I had neither the speed nor the strength to excel in football. My inability to hit a curve ball abbreviated a collegiate baseball career. My only participation in track was in high school, but that was a fledgling enterprise. So I grew up with average athletic skills but with a tremendous interest in sports and with a great appreciation for the lessons I learned by participating in athletics.

Pierre De Coubertin, who was chiefly responsible for the revival of the Olympic games in the late nineteenth century, observed, "The important thing in the Olympic games is not to win but to take part, the important thing in life is not the triumph but the struggle. The essential thing is not to have conquered but to have fought well. To spread these precepts is to build up a stronger and more valiant and, above all, more scrupulous and more generous humanity."[1]

There were things I learned by participating in sports that I never could have learned in the classroom. The discipline, the mental toughness, the hard work demanded by some of my coaches instilled in me the importance of commitment, diligence, teamwork, physical fitness, and goal setting. In athletics I learned to lose with dignity and win with grace. I was motivated to participate in athletics by some of the great sports figures of the 1940s and 1950s. They were my heroes.

One of my first heroes was Ted Williams, the "Splendid Splinter" of the Boston Red Sox. Some of my happiest memories from my childhood revolve around trips to Washington, D.C., to watch the Red Sox play the Washington Senators in old Griffith Park. My dad was a Red Sox fan and took me to the nation's capital to see the likes of Mel Parnell, Dom DiMaggio, Johnny Pesky, Walt Dropo, and, of course, the "kid," Ted Williams. The family's allegiance to the Bosox now spans three generations. In fact, on a recent trip back from Boston, my son John and his wife, Kathryn, brought me a commemorative picture set of Williams. This treasured keepsake occupies a prominent place on the wall behind my desk.

I contend that Williams was the greatest hitter in baseball history. While baseball continued during the Second World War and the Korean War, Williams served two stints of duty in the marine corps as a fighter pilot. By fulfilling his duties as a patriotic American, he gave up five years of playing time at the peak of his profession. I did not appreciate some of Williams's antics on the field, and I did not like his general disdain for the press, but he was one of my heroes, and I admired him because of his proficiency in hitting a baseball and his devotion to his country.

The athletes who added character to their list of credentials seemed to escalate on my scale of heroes. When I played high school football I had a newspaper clipping about Bill Glass taped to the inside of my locker. Glass, an All-America football player at Baylor University, was a devout Christian and had an outstanding career in the NFL with the Cleveland Browns. His courageous stand for Christ had a powerful impact upon my life as a teenager.

Bobby Richardson, second baseman for the New York Yankees, was another of my heroes, even though the Yankees have always been the nemesis of the Red Sox. But Richardson's steadfast witness for Christ made him one of my heroes.

An Olympian for whom I had great admiration in the 1950s was Bob Richards, a theology professor from Laverne, California. Richards won the bronze medal in the pole vault in the 1948 games in London and the gold medal in the 1952 Helsinki games and in the 1956 Melbourne games. Richards, known as the Vaulting Vicar, is the only person to win two gold medals and three overall medals in the pole vault.[2] Richards believed that the redeemed of the Lord should become heralds for the cause of Christ. His medals not only signified that he was an Olympic champion but that he was also a champion for Christ.

Not all heroes are Olympic champions or superstars in the world of sports. You, in fact, may be someone's hero. Someone who admires you greatly may be watching every move you make, but you may never know who is following in your steps.

I rarely forget birthdays and anniversaries, but for some reason there is one date I will always remember: July 20, 1969. It was during the wee hours of the morning, and I had been watching Neil Armstrong, commander of the Apollo 11 mission, taking the first steps on the surface of the moon.

After having vicariously shared the exhilaration and the emotion of that experience, I fell asleep on the sofa. Suddenly I was awakened by the sound of someone's shuffling down the hallway of our home. I knew immediately that it was not my wife, because the heavy plodding that I heard on the hardwood floor in no way resembled her footsteps. Our two-year-old daughter, Miriam, was the only other person in residence, so I began to brace myself for the intruder who had apparently invaded our home.

My adrenaline was flowing. My blood pressure was rising. A flood of thoughts raced through my mind—all terribly frightening. I began groping for anything I could use for a weapon. Poised for action, all of a sudden I heard the voice of my two-year-old. "Hi, daddy. Whatcha doin'?"

In that instant I fell back on the couch as limp as a rag doll. Although I had been stunned into silence, Miriam asked again, "Daddy, whatcha doin'?"

As she made her way around the side of the chair, showing her full thirty-inch frame, I saw by the light of the television that she was wearing my wing-tipped shoes.

"What am I doing?" I gasped. "The question is, What are you doing? What are you doing with my shoes? I thought you were some big bad robber coming to get me."

With a smile of innocence, Miriam said, "Daddy, I no robber. I just walkin' awound in your shoes."

You may not be an Olympic hero, but you are undoubtedly someone's hero. Whether you realize it or not, you are a person of influence. If someone chooses to walk around in your shoes or follow in your steps, will they be walking in the pathway of integrity or tottering down the road to destruction? In terms of influencing the character development of others, you have the potential of being a curse or a blessing, a stumbling block or a steppingstone. Remember the words of the psalmist: "The steps of a good man are ordered by the LORD" (Ps. 37:23). Walk in such a way that the most impressionable child will not err by following in your steps.

In this book you will discover the significance of Olympic symbols and meet some Olympic heroes. You will be familiar with some, and perhaps you will encounter some for the very first time. These men and women have different faces and come from different places, but they've all been heroes in the eyes of multitudes of people. Perhaps you will find your own heroes in the pages that follow. Most of these Olympians are exemplary in many ways, but they are all world-class athletes and proven winners. Just remember that the greatest athlete, although he may have swift feet, coordinated feet, nimble feet, strong feet, also has feet of clay. Hopefully, your ultimate hero is the one whose feet did not fall or falter even though they had been pierced with nails.

The Olympic Motto

The Olympic motto is *Citius, Altius, Fortius,* or "Faster, Higher, Stronger." These words have inspired and motivated Olympic athletes throughout the years. This is a call to excellence. It is a call to scale heights, broaden horizons, reset standards, beat the clock, and better the best.

Citius is the Latin word for "faster." Some would say that today's synthetic tracks and starting blocks have helped modern-day runners perform faster. Others would credit better-conditioned athletes and more knowledgeable coaches. Still others contend that the grooming process of today's athletes begins at an earlier age than before. Statistics don't lie, however, and the numbers show that the pace is faster than ever in Olympic track events.

I am a product of the 1950s. During that fabulous-but-sometimes-frivolous decade, I was a miler on our high school track team. I was also the first baseman for the Valdese North Carolina Tigers. After the last class period we would hustle to the gymnasium to dress for the afternoon baseball practice. For those who played in the infield, practice consisted of fielding countless ground balls. There were ground balls to the right, ground balls to the left, hard ones, high hoppers—continuous ground balls. Then the infielders would whip the old horsehide around the horn in all kinds of variations, in endless repetition. Batting practice was a delight, but all too brief, because it was followed by running the bases and occasionally wind sprints—ugh!

After baseball practice, those of us on the track team had to run even more. Running, running, running—perspiration flowing, muscles aching, dehydration ensuing, stomach churning, mind wondering, *Does this coach have a bent toward masochism?*

Every lap around the 440 track seemed like a mile.

Every day the challenge was to run harder, go faster, beat the previous day's time. "Faster, faster," was the perpetual cry.

I remember laboring around those last laps as if a ball and chain were attached to each ankle. On the far turn of the track and at the greatest distance from the coach's watchful eye, we slowed our pace and plodded along trying to get a second wind. The coach constantly challenged us, saying, "Mediocrity never mastered anything but mediocrity, and excellence is achieved not through ease, but effort —exceptional effort."

At the spring track meet that year in Hickory, North Carolina, I summoned every nerve, sinew, muscle, ligament, ounce of my body, and fiber of my being and finished the mile in 5 minutes 51 seconds. Roger Bannister had just broken the 4-minute mile a few years earlier, and such a feat seemed incredible to me.

The race most comparable to the mile in the Olympics is the 1,500 meters. Edwin Flack, a twenty-two-year-old accountant from Australia,[3] won this prestigious race at the first modern Olympic games in Athens in 1896 with a time of 4 minutes 33.2 seconds.[4] Throughout the years, men and women have run faster and set new records in this race. In the 1992 Summer Games in Barcelona, Hasfiba Boulmerka of Algeria won this race in the women's event with a time of 3 minutes 55.3 seconds. The men's winner was Fermin Cacho of Spain with a time of 3 minutes 40.12 seconds. Sebastian Coe of Great Britain holds the Olympic record for the 1,500 meters with a time of 3 minutes 32.53 seconds in the 1984 games in Los Angeles.[5]

Coe's record is the standard, the goal, that future Olympic athletes are striving to break, motivated by the Olympic motto. Better-trained, better-disciplined, and better-equipped athletes will forever compete for a faster pace and an improved time and a new record.

Altius is the Latin word for "higher." Basketball players are increasing their vertical jump with each passing decade. High jumpers continue to set new marks as they soar to new elevations year after year. The pole vaulters almost seem to defy the law of gravity as they hurl themselves over those precariously perched bars extended ever higher and higher. These physical achievements, however, serve only to illustrate the high ideals that are inspired by the Olympic games.

I recently visited El Salvador, the most densely populated nation in the Western Hemisphere. I found the people friendly and hard working. I was interested in El Salvador's past participation in the Olympic games. Although they had occasionally sent a handful of athletes to these international events, no El Salvadorian had ever won a medal.

El Salvador sent six athletes to the 1988 games in Seoul, Korea. The only male athlete in the track-and-field events was Jim Mellado, who participated in the decathlon competition. Ten months after my trip to El Salvador, I met this splendid young man in Chicago. At five-feet eight-inches and 160 pounds, he did not look like the typical decathlon athlete.

Jim had attended Southern Methodist University on a track scholarship. He was an intense competitor and trained for the intermediate hurdles, the high jump, and the long jump. Yet at the coach's suggestion he began to prepare for the decathlon.

Jim welcomed the challenge, because he had always been inspired by the athletic prowess of Bruce Jenner, the decathlon champion of the 1976 Olympics in Montreal. In only his second decathlon competition at SMU, Jim set a school record with 7,100 points.

This muscular young Central American won the right to represent El Salvador in the 1988 Olympic games by placing fourth in the Pan American Games in Indianapolis in 1987. Jim then returned to Dallas to work with his college coach at SMU to prepare for Seoul.

Of the ten decathlon events, I was most interested in asking Jim about the pole vault. He replied, "It's all about speed and power. You've really got to get a head of steam going down the runway, get an early plant, whip your body up, invert, and over the bar."[6]

The speed, strength, and technique of pole vaulters permit them to go higher and higher. In 1896 William Welles Hoyt of the United States won the gold medal in Athens, Greece, with a jump of 10 feet 10 inches.[7] Today the current world-record holder in the pole vault, Sergei Bubka of the former Soviet Union, and gold medalist in Seoul in 1988, has scaled a height of more than twenty feet several times.

Is the sky the limit for pole vaulters? Although they will continue to jump higher and higher in years to come, they will always find the battle with gravity a tremendous challenge to overcome.

To the Latin words *citius* and *altius,* we add the word *fortius,* completing the Olympic motto. This word is defined as "stronger." Where in the Olympic venue do you go to find an example of strength? Weightlifting?

You could look at the hulking power lifters and see an example of strength and fortitude. But almost every Olympic event requires a measure of strength. Would you expect to find an example of strength in a natitorium among women divers? Indeed, they must have an incredible amount of strength and endurance to be successful in major competition.

When I was a boy, I thought diving consisted of standing atop Eagle Rock, twenty feet above the "black hole" in the Catawba River, holding your nose, closing your eyes, and just "jumpin'." As the years passed and as I watched some of the Olympic divers on television, I began to realize that there was more to "real" diving than just "jumpin'."

Lee Ann Fletcher-Cox, a two-time collegiate all-American diver, competed in the U.S. Olympic Festival in Minneapolis in 1990. Her training regimen began at 5:15 A.M. every morning. She worked out two hours before school, engaged in rehab every afternoon, and then practiced another two to three hours, not only diving, but swimming countless laps to increase her endurance. Training also included time on a stationary bike, a stairmaster, and a trampoline daily.

Workouts in the weight room were a vital part of the stringent discipline required to increase her strength. When I met Lee Ann, I was thoroughly impressed by her program of aerobics, abdonimals, and plyometrics. In fact, I had never even heard the word *plyometrics* before. I came to realize that it is an intensive training program designed to enhance one's leaping ability. Plyometrics develops the muscles that will thrust a diver upward and outward with explosive power.

Lee Ann does not look like she belongs in the woman's division of the American Gladiators. In fact, she's quite petite. But because of her training regimen, she excels in strength.

Every four years the Olympic Games provide a new benchmark in strength as the participants prove themselves to be *fortius et fortius.* If records are meant to be broken, the Olympics prove it. There is something about the human spirit that calls us to new frontiers, to conquer new worlds, to expand our horizons, and to beat the best.

Citius, Altius, Fortius is all about aspiration, achievement, and excellence. The apostle Paul would refer to it as "pressing toward the mark."

It is only right that the Olympics inspire and demand excellence. So does the Lord of heaven. In the Sermon on the Mount, Jesus said, "Be ye therefore perfect, even as your Father which is in heaven is perfect" (Matt. 5:48). Surely God deserves our best, but so often we give Him the odd moments of our time, the ragged edge of our talents, and a trifling trickle of our treasure.

In the Book of Malachi, the people of Judah were reprimanded for bringing blemished animals as sacrifices to the Lord. "'When you bring injured, crippled or diseased animals and offer them as sacrifices, should I accept them from your hands?' says the Lord. 'Cursed is the cheat who has an acceptable male in his flock and vows to give it, but then sacrifices a blemished animal to the Lord. For I am a great king,' says the Lord Almighty, 'and my name is to be feared among the nations'" (Mal. 1:13b–14, NIV). Surely, the majestic God of the universe deserves our best.

If the motto of the Olympics is *Citius, Altius, Fortius,* the motto of Christians should be *semper verus, semper probus, semper fidelis,* or "always true, always obedient, always faithful."

The Olympic Torch

On the credenza in my study is a statue of a man and woman in running attire carrying a torch. I won it for the only bright spot in my not-so-illustrious golfing career. I keep the trophy, not so much as a reminder of my nearest-to-the-pin prize, but as a reminder of the great significance of the Olympic torch.

As nearly as I can determine, the statue is a replica of a sculptured work by Marcel Jovine. I am not a connoisseur of art, but my guess is that the statue represents Steve Prefontaine and Sandra Henderson who carried the Olympic torch into the stadium for the opening ceremonies of the 1972 Montreal games.

Have you ever held a torch in your hand? Such flames of fire have held significance and purpose for millenniums. The torch has sometimes stood for wisdom and knowledge, at other times it has been the symbol for freedom. According to Greek mythology, Zeus devised a plan to destroy mankind by depriving the earth of fire. Prometheus thwarted Zeus' plan by stealing fire from the gods and giving it to human beings. If there is any truth to be derived from mythology, it is only that fire is a gift from above and, like most things, has the potential of being used either to bless or curse mankind.[8]

When I think of torches or flames of fire, I also think of Indiana Jones. As I watched that trilogy of action-adventure movies starring Harrison Ford, I was captivated by Indiana, an indomitable adventurer, an undaunted soldier of fortune. He was always in search of some forbidden prize: the ark of the covenant, the holy grail, or the piece of map that would complete the trail to some mysterious treasure trove.

In his quests, he repeatedly extricated himself miraculously from death-threatening dilemmas. In one scene this grand adventurer was trapped in a subterranean passageway infested with rats. He found his way out, however, with the light of a torch.

While the guiding flame of Indiana Jones fulfilled its purpose, the eternal flame in Arlington Cemetery fulfills yet another. How well do I remember November 22, 1963. My wife and I lived in Wake Forest, North Carolina, at the time. It was a cool, pleasant day in that sleepy little town. I was playing basketball in the seminary gymnasium when the news came that John F. Kennedy had been shot. Then came the horrifying news from Parkland Hospital in Dallas, Texas, that the president was dead, felled by an assassin's bullet.

The thirty-fifth president of the United States was buried with full military honors at Arlington National Cemetery near the nation's capitol. At the conclusion of the funeral service, Jacqueline Kennedy lighted an eternal flame to burn at the site of the grave. The flame burns today to signify the light and leadership of this vigorous, dynamic president.

While Indiana Jones's torch lighted the way for his adventure, and while the eternal flame in Arlington National Cemetery provokes memories of the past, the torch of the Statue of Liberty symbolizes receptivity and welcome. American poet Emma Lazarus highlighted the significance of the torch with her sonnet, entitled "The New Colossus." This beautiful verse was engraved on a bronze tablet and affixed to the pedestal of the statue.

> Not like the brazen giant of Greek fame,
> With conquering limbs astride from land to land:
> Here at our sea-washed, sunset gates shall stand
> A mighty woman with a torch, whose flame
> Is the imprisoned lightening, and her name
> Mother of Exiles. From her beacon-hand
> Glows world-wide welcome[9]

Flames that guide, flames that cause us to remember, and flames of receptivity and welcome. The spirit of the Statue of Liberty and the spirit of the Olympic games are amazingly similar. As the torch of Lady Liberty, the torch of the Olympics "glows world-wide welcome." On April 6, 1995, the Atlanta Organizing Committee for the Centennial Games presented the torch that will carry the Olympic flame from ancient Olympia in Greece to Atlanta to open the 1996 summer games. Billy Payne, president of the committee, said, "In presenting this torch, I want to thank Greece for its gift to the world, the Olympic movement. It is the single idea in this world which calls on all people to unite."

Prior to the games, the torch, a modern invention dating only from 1936, is taken to Olympia, a sanctuary of Greek mythology and the site of the ancient Olympic games. It is ignited by rays from the sun and transported by relay to the opening ceremony.

The opening ceremony is a singular event, marked by a parade of the athletes who, dressed in distinctive athletic uniforms, march in national groups behind their flags. The procession of nations is led by the athletes of Greece, always positioned as the first to march into the stadium. This tradition began as an homage to the original Olympics held in ancient Greece. The athletes of the other nations follow in alphabetical order by country. The procession is concluded with the athletes of the host nation.

As the athletes stand in impressive array before the assembled throng, a hush settles over the stadium in anticipation of the pronouncement, "Let the games begin!" which is generally made by the host country's chief of state. The pronouncement is punctuated with a cannonade. The Olympic flag is ceremoniously unfurled. Trumpets herald that the games have begun. Doves and pigeons are released as a symbol of goodwill and peace.

Everything that happens in the opening ceremonies leads to the climactic moment when the Olympic flame is ignited. Hundreds, sometimes thousands of relay runners combine to bring the lighted torch into the stadium from Greece. These runners represent each country that lies between Greece and the host nation. Planes and ships transport the flame across deserts, mountains, and seas. In anticipation of the final runner entering the stadium, every eye is riveted on the entrance area. As the torch is carried into the arena, a welcoming response swells as the runner circles the track, reaching a crescendo when the the torch ignites the Olympic flame. The flame is kept burning throughout the celebration, signifying that peace should prevail—at least until the closing ceremony.[10]

The first torch used in the modern Olympics appeared in Berlin in 1936. Those opening ceremonies were marked by pomp and splendor. Three thousand relay runners representing seven different nationalities carried the torch from the sacred grove in Olympia. The last runner carried the flaming torch past the ordered ranks of thousands of German soldiers and swastika banners. At last, with the Olympic torch blazing at the opened end of the magnificent stadium, thousands of doves were released and the games began.[11]

The Fifteenth Olympiad was held in Helsinki, Finland, in 1952. The torch was carried by foot runners to Athens from Olympia, flown by plane to Denmark, and transported by ferryboat from Copenhagen to Malmo, Sweden. Relay runners carried the torch through Stockholm, where motorcyclists and motorists took it to the Finnish border. In Finland the torch was carried entirely by the nation's athletes until it was brought triumphantly into the Helsinki stadium. Paavo Nurmi, winner of seven Olympic gold medals, circled the track amid great adulation. The flaming torch was then passed to Hannes Kolehmainen, a sports legend in

Scandinavia, who took it to the tower of the stadium to light the Olympic flame.[12]

In 1964, Yoshinori Sakai of Waseda University carried the torch into the Tokyo stadium to mark the beginning of the Eighteenth Olympiad. Sakai was not known for his athletic prowess, but he had been selected because he symbolized to the world the hope for a peaceful future. Sakai had been born near Hiroshima on August 6, 1945, the day an atomic bomb exploded over that city.[13]

In 1968, the Olympic torch was transported from Greece to Spain and then by ship to Mexico. The ship followed the course of Christopher Columbus's first voyage to the New World. Enrequita Basilio, a hurdler, delivered the torch into the stadium to ignite the Olympic flame. It was the first time a woman had been so honored.[14]

In 1972, in Munich, 8,000 athletes from 121 nations marched into the stadium as part of the opening ceremony. The torch arrived accompanied by runners from each continent. Jim Ryun represented North America. Guenter Zahn carried the torch and lit the flame.[15]

In the Twenty-first Olympiad in Montreal, Canada, in 1976, the torch was carried into the stadium by the two young athletes I believe are represented in my statue—Stephen Prefontaine and Sandra Henderson. Presumably, this was the first time that the Olympic torch had been carried into the stadium by two individuals.[16]

In the summer of 1984, a plane brought the torch from Olympia to New York. It was carried across America "kilometer by kilometer, runner by runner, from sea to shining sea."[17] From New York the route included more than one thousand cities and towns and found its way through thirty-three states.

The response to the sight of the torch was incredible. People removed their hats and placed their hands over their hearts as if they were pledging allegiance to the flag. Some clapped their hands with delight. Many sang patriotic songs. Trumpets blared. Church bells rang. Sirens sounded. Some people threw flowers in the pathway of the runners. Children stayed up to see the torch carried through their town or hamlet. People left their jobs to line the streets where the torchbearer would pass. Truckers sounded their horns. Shouts of encouragement to the runners were commonplace all the way to the Los Angeles Coliseum, where ninety-three thousand people erupted in one gigantic, convulsive cheer.

The torch's path across America was stitched into the typography like a thread of gold, inspiring togetherness and unity. The *Los Angeles Times* reported that the torch "linked ancient past and present, one country and another, sport and sportsmanship. But most stunning of all, that flame of international harmony bound together Americans in one exultant patriotic hurrah."[18]

On February 9, 1994, just three days before the Winter Olympics in Lillehammer, Norway, Michael Finkel awaited his turn to run with the Olympic torch. His assignment: Leg 28 in the route designed by the Lillehammer Olympic Committee. He was one of seventy-five hundred people who had been selected to participate in the seventy-five-day, five-thousand-mile lap around Norway. With the circuit several days away from completion, more than 50 percent of the country's 4.3 million people had watched the torch pass. Finkel was to carry the torch only five hundred meters and then pass it off to the next runner, but somehow the significance of participating in the great event was overwhelming. More than one hundred thousand applications had been sent to the Olympic Organizing Committee, but Finkel was one of the chosen few. He said, "I knew that just about everyone in Norway would have traded their finest reindeer-skin rug for the opportunity to . . . carry the Olympic torch for a few minutes."[19]

The torch for the 1996 games is made of aluminum, wood, brass, and gold. Antonio Tzikas, president of the Greek Olympic Committee, noted, "Many cities will want to be a part of the torch relay, but I can tell you the relay will be longer than any of the past." Once again the privilege of being a part of the torch relay is an honor coveted by tens of thousands. Volunteers from all over the country are offering their services for this cherished responsibility. Who wouldn't want to carry a torch symbolizing international peace and goodwill among the nations?

Followers of Christ carry a light of eternal significance that will never burn out. We have the privilege of holding forth the light of the gospel and becoming living flames of witness for His cause of forgiveness and love. Our source of light is none other than Jesus Christ. We are illuminated by Him. As believers we are reflections of His glory. He is as the sun, and we are as the moon. Our light is a derived light. Therefore, the closer we are to Him and the more intimate our relationship with Him, the more we are able to reflect the brilliance of His light.

Jesus said, "You are the light of the world. . . . Let your light so shine before men, that they may see your good works, and glorify your Father which is in heaven" (Matt. 5:14, 16).

The Olympic Flag

The Olympic games have an official flag that is beautifully symbolic and universally recognized as emblematic of the world's premier athletic extravaganza. Just as the shape of the Coca-Cola bottle identifies its producer, just as the golden arches represent McDonald's, just as a charging bull represents an upswing in the stock market, just as "the Fighting Irish" suggests the Notre Dame football team, the Olympic flag has become the insignia for those special games that claim the world's attention every four years. Just as each country has its own flag, so the Olympic Games has a flag that represents all of the nations, the races, and the languages of the world.

In July 1995, my wife and I accompanied our church's high school choir to Nassau, on New Providence Island, in the Commonwealth of the Bahamas. We found the Bahamian people to be every bit as gracious and hospitable as southerners in the United States are reputed to be. We were treated as royalty.

While there, we were introduced to the Bahamian Games in progress at the time. The people were obviously interested in these exciting contests. The media gave excellent coverage throughout the competition. The people expressed a fervent interest in practically every event and carefully noted the performance of their favorite sports personalities. Even on the streets, conversations included speculations as to who would represent this country in the 1996 Olympic Games.

As the Bahamian Games progressed, a spirit of pride and patriotism seemed to permeate the entire country. The flag of this commonwealth, representing twenty-two years of independence, was unfurled in many places across the island. It was obvious that this banner of freedom had great significance for the citizens of New Providence.

The Bahamian flag has three horizontal stripes of equal width. The bottom and top stripes are light blue, and the center stripe is yellow. A black triangle lies with its base along the hoist and its apex in the central yellow stripe. The light blue stripe at the top represents the sky, and the bottom blue stripe represents the sea. The yellow stripe is emblematic of the sun, and the black triangle represents the people. The flag also serves as a symbol of unity and peace in the nation.

We can be sure that when the Bahamian athletes enter the Olympic stadium in Atlanta for the opening ceremony, they will carry their national banner with pride. Indeed, the athletes of every nation will march into the stadium in pomp and splendor with flags proudly unfurled as the games' festivities begin.

The parade of nations will begin, of course, with Greece, carrying its standard with nine horizontal stripes of sky blue and white, bearing a white cross. The athletes of the United States will form the rear guard of the parade of nations, holding forth the Star Spangled Banner. All of the other participating nations will march into the stadium in alphabetical order with their flags aloft.

The primary insignia for the centennial games, however, will be the Olympic flag, one of the most visible and recognized emblems in the world today. This flag consists of a white field and five centered rings, three rings side by side, but not intertwined, and two rings below which hook through the three above. The top three rings are, from left to right, blue, black, and red. The bottom two are yellow and green.

The five-ringed emblem on the flag was inspired by five interlocking rings that appear on an altar in Delphi, one of the city-states of ancient Greece. It was a meeting place for those attempting the political unification of all Greek peoples. One of the ingredients of the master plan to accomplish this unification was the establishment of the Panhellenic Pythian games. The friendly competition of such athletic events would surely remove barriers of division and build bridges of unity.[20]

The altar at Delphi bearing the five interlocking rings has a history. Many believe that this emblem was borrowed from the sacred discus of Iphitus, which was marked by five similar rings symbolizing truce and peace. King Iphitus of Elis ruled around 884 B.C. It was during his reign that everyone's safety was guaranteed during their ancient games. No one was allowed to take up arms. All legal disputes were suspended. No death penalties were carried out while the games were in progress.[21]

Likewise, during the Olympics, the torch burns brightly throughout the games, and the Olympic flag flies majestically above the site of each Olympic event. These powerful symbols issue a clarion call to peace on earth. Indeed, the games inspire a spirit of international community. For a brief moment every few years in the course of history, there is one flag that is common to many nations and multitudes of people.

In the United States, every state in the union has its own flag. However, the flags of the individual states are secondary to the Stars and Stripes—the U.S. flag. In some similar fashion, the Olympic flag reigns supreme over the Olympic village, and the national flags seem to wave in support of the Olympic effort rather than signal a spirit of independence.

Baron Pierre De Coubertin, founder of the International Olympic Committee in 1894, served as the president of the IOC from 1896 to 1916 and again from 1919 to 1925. He was a French idealist who envisioned the rebirth of the ancient games as a means of developing well-rounded individuals and building "up a stronger and more valiant and, above all, more scrupulous and more generous humanity."

De Coubertin recognized and appreciated the symbolism embodied in the five interlocking rings of Delphi and used them to design the Olympic flag, which made its debut in 1914 in Paris at the celebration of the twentieth anniversary of the revival of the games. However, the Olympic flag was not used as part of an Olympiad until the 1920 games in Antwerp, Belgium.

Through the years, rings have had great significance. Sometimes they were the insignia of authority. At other times they were used for the purpose of betrothal or to signify an engagement. Wedding rings symbolize the covenant that has been established between a husband and wife. Ecclesiastical rings are ceremonially worn, signifying the marriage of the wearer to the church. In days long ago it was the custom to bequeath memorial rings to one's friends. Typically, rings symbolize a relationship of unity and oneness. The unbroken circle of the ring symbolizes the lasting qualities of an abiding relationship.

The five rings in the Olympic flag stand for the five original continents represented in the early games: Europe, Asia, Africa, Oceana, and the Americas. The fact that they are interlocked can be thought to mean two things—the union of the five continents that compete in the games and the meeting of the athletes from around the world in a spirit of fair competition.[22] The colors of the rings were chosen because at least one of them appears in the flag of every nation in the Olympic movement.

Everyone needs a motto to live by, a song to sing, and a banner of identification. David the psalmist declared, "We will rejoice in thy salvation, and in the name of our God we will set up our banners: the LORD fulfil all thy petitions" (Ps. 20:5).

The Olympic flag has great significance and fulfills a beautiful purpose in our world today. The flags of the nations are colorful and inspire national pride and patriotism. What banner best represents your life? Consider for your life the banner of the cross of Christ.

> There's a royal banner given for display
> To the soldiers of the King.
> As an ensign fair we lift it up today,
> While as ransomed ones we sing.
> Marching on, marching on,
> For Christ count everything but loss!
> And to crown Him king, we'll toil and sing
> 'Neath the banner of the cross!

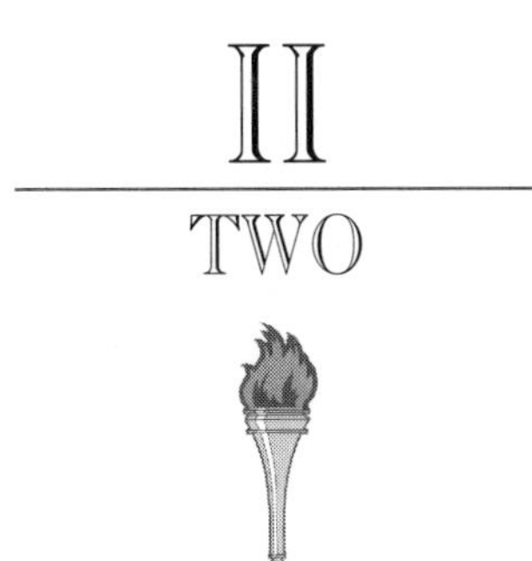

The World's Strongest Man

Paul Anderson

Luciano Pavarotti singing with the Grand Ole Opry on stage at the old Ryman Theater in Nashville, Tennessee, would appear somewhat unusual. Similarly, no one would expect to see funny man Steve Martin playing Hamlet at the Winter Garden Theater in New York City. To me, Paul Anderson looked equally out of place in a church pulpit, but that's where I first saw him.

Those whom I had seen in the pulpit were typically balding, middle-aged, bespectacled men speaking in pious tones. Never had I seen an "incredible hulk" like Paul Anderson in the pulpit. His presence was captivating. This modern-day Samson was only five feet, ten and a half inches tall, but through weight training he had grown to 375 pounds. He had a twenty-three-and-one-half-inch neck, twenty-two-and-one-half-inch upper arms, a fifty-eight-inch chest, thirty-five-inch thighs, and twenty-inch calves. Yet this man with grizzly bear strength had the tenderness of a teddy bear. He had an amazing love for people, especially kids, and he always declared that God was the source of his strength.

Anderson's feats of strength are well documented. He took up weightlifting as part of his football training at Furman University. He played his freshman year as a scholarship athlete and went home for the Christmas holidays never to return.

"Why won't you go back to school?" he was asked.

"They are starving us to death," he lamented.

In 1954 in Washington, Anderson became the first man to exceed 1,000 pounds in the Olympic lifts with a 375-pound press, a 320-pound snatch, and a 405-pound jerk.

The press, discontinued as an Olympic event after the 1972 games in Munich, requires the lifter to bring the bar to his shoulders, then push it slowly above his head using only his arms. The snatch is accomplished by lifting the bar overhead from the floor in one single sweeping motion. The jerk is performed in two parts. First, the bar is lifted from the floor to the shoulders, then, with a quick stiffening of the legs, jerked above the head using the combined strength of both arms and legs.

Anderson astonished the sports world on June 15, 1955, during a meet in Moscow. Before fifteen thousand stunned spectators, he pressed 402 pounds and jerked 425.5 pounds, establishing world records with both lifts. The Soviet announcer exclaimed in amazement, "A wonder of nature!"[1]

The desire to participate in the 1956 Olympics in Melbourne, Australia, grew in Paul's heart. The call from "down under" could not be resisted. Although the Olympic Games will return to Australia—in Sydney—in the year 2000, only once before, in 1956, has this colossal event been held in the Southern Hemisphere. Because of the reversed seasons, the Summer Games in Melbourne were held from November 22 through December 8.

The super heavyweight division of the weightlifting event in Melbourne was supposed to be a cakewalk for Anderson. He developed strep throat, however, and was not at his best physically. Humberto Selvetti of Argentina posed a formidable threat to the American champion. After two of the three events, Selvetti was ahead by 7.5 kilograms. In the jerk, the Argentinean challenged Anderson by succeeding in his lift with 180 kilograms.

Anderson called for 187.5 kilograms, just the weight needed to better his opponent. He had three chances to win the gold medal. His throat burning as if seared with a hot poker, beads of perspiration appearing on his fevered brow, the native of Toccoa, Georgia, failed in his first two attempts. As he prepared for his third and final effort, he knew that in his weakened condition he would have to call on a source of strength other than his own. With a heroic effort he succeeded in lifting the bar from the floor to his shoulders. Then, with a prayer in his heart and a refusal to fail, he stiffened his legs. With a mighty, perhaps supernatural surge of strength, he pushed the bar (413.25 pounds) up, up, up. His grimace mirrored his determination. His arms locked. His legs moved to a parallel position. The judges signaled a legitimate lift.

Actually, Anderson had only matched the weight lifted by Selvetti. But since Anderson had lost sixty pounds getting in shape for the Olympics, at 303.25 pounds he weighed less than Selvetti and won the gold medal.[2]

Additional stunts demonstrating incredible power lay ahead for the gold medalist. In June 1957 he pushed the limits of his strength and raised 6,270 pounds with his back. According to the *Guinness Book of Records,* that was the greatest weight ever raised by a human being. On *The Ed Sullivan Show,* he raised a carousel bearing children on live ponies.

Weightlifting was the medium Anderson used to attract his audience and enhance his real purpose in life. He felt that God had called him to establish homes for deprived and needy youths. In the church where I heard him encourage his hearers to build a life of faith and integrity, he also gave a demonstration of his physical strength. With eight high school athletes sitting on a table, Anderson lifted the table.

The pulpit was as familiar to Anderson as the weight room. In fact, he preached in so many pulpits the Methodist Conference of South Georgia made him a licensed minister. He was particularly effective in providing direction and encouragement to troubled teenagers. In talking with judges and law enforcement officers, he discovered that there was no wholesome place for many of these youths to live.

This great man with a compassionate heart decided to respond to this need by founding the Paul Anderson Youth Home in Vidalia, Georgia. Other Paul Anderson homes have opened in Dallas and Washington.

So often the younger generation is criticized for their music, their fads, their fashion, their propensities, and a myriad of things. Many adults with a gloomy counsel, an unforgiving spirit, and a negative countenance get into an elder brother syndrome and quench the spirit of youth. How refreshing to see the Paul Andersons of this world who eagerly extend a helping hand to the younger generation.

Oh, remember those eight high school athletes on that table I saw Anderson lift with his back? He spent his whole life doing exactly that—lifting up hurting and fallen and needy youths.

Paul Anderson died on August 15, 1994, at sixty-one years of age. A childhood kidney ailment recurred in June

1982. He had a kidney transplant the following year, and his body that had achieved countless feats of strength was wracked by numerous ailments following the surgery. At the time of his death, the former world's strongest man weighed less than two hundred pounds.

Pat Williams, general manager of the NBA Orlando Magic, said, "Just as there is only one Babe Ruth and one Mohammed Ali, there will be only one Paul Anderson. We've lost a great pioneer athlete and human being." Yes, and we have all lost a man whose heart was always bigger than his bulging muscles.

God is primarily interested in the issues of the heart. God's Word declares that "man looketh on the outward appearance, but the LORD looketh on the heart" (1 Sam. 16:7b). The development of strong bodies with sinewy muscles is commendable, but the inward man must never be neglected. The days of the strongest of men are numbered, and time ultimately neutralizes the benefits of any weightlifting program. The issues of the heart, however, are eternal. The apostle Paul wrote, "but though our outward man perish, yet the inward man is renewed day by day. . . . We look not at the things which are seen, but at the things which are not seen: for the things which are seen are temporal; but the things which are not seen are eternal" (2 Cor. 4:16, 18).

Bamboozled

Yuri Vlasov

A friend saw a brochure advertising land for sale in New Mexico. These one-half-acre lots were described as a veritable paradise situated in the midst of a verdant oasis. Five years after he had purchased the property, while visiting in the southwestern part of the country, he decided to visit his little slice of utopia. What he found was not paradise but an undeveloped region of sand, rocks, cactus, and Gila monsters. You can well imagine his reaction upon discovering that he had invested a considerable sum of money in a barren wasteland. He felt misused and abused. Deceived! Defrauded! Duped! Bamboozled!

That's how Yuri Vlasov felt in the 1964 Olympics in Tokyo. Vlasov, representing the Soviet Union, had won the gold medal in weightlifting's superheavyweight division in the 1960 games in Rome. He not only defeated his primary opponents—James Bradford and Norbert Schemansky of the United States—but he also beat Paul Anderson's world record by 11.5 pounds (4.5 kilograms).

After leaving Rome clothed in laurels and victory, Vlasov decided to quit his lifting and devote himself to the passion of his life: writing poetry. Although some of his works were highly acclaimed, he was not able to market his work successfully. He found it impossible to make ends meet financially. Therefore, by necessity, he returned to weightlifting. He began to focus his attention upon preparing for the 1964 Tokyo games.

The games made their way to Asia for the first time that year. Tokyo had been awarded the Twelfth Olympiad in 1940 to coincide with the nation's twenty-six hundreth birthday, but World War II canceled those plans. The choice to host the Seventeenth Olympiad, however, was welcomed enthusiastically throughout the nation. The people of Japan went to great lengths to prove to the world that they had completely recovered from the devastation of the war. More than $3 billion was spent in Tokyo alone to refurbish the city in preparation for the games. A record number of nations (ninety-three) were represented in this Olympiad that was referred to as the "Happy Games." Vlasov, however, did not find the Tokyo games to be an occasion for personal joy.[1]

Having failed in his attempt to support himself through his writing, Vlasov dedicated himself to winning another gold medal for the Soviet Union. He trained arduously and established another world record prior to the Tokyo games, setting the benchmark for combined lifts at 580 kilograms.

In Tokyo, Vlasov found his major competition was a teammate from the Ukraine, 341-pound Leonid Zhabotinsky. Vlasov outlifted Zhabotinsky in the press by 10 kilograms.

In the snatch, the massive Ukrainian won by 5 kilograms, but Vlasov was still comfortably ahead with his best event, the jerk, yet to come. Not only did Vlasov hold the world record for the three combined lifts, but he held the world's record for the jerk.

Prior to the jerk, with Vlasov in the lead, Zhabotinsky conceded defeat. He walked up to Yuri and said, "Congratulations. I will never defeat you in the final lift. You are the world champion. You hold the world's record. You shall win the gold medal. I shall be satisfied to win the silver medal for the Soviet team." Zhabotinsky lulled Vlasov into a false sense of security. Consequently, the world recordholder approached the final event with a slight degree of complacency. He had lost his focus, his concentration, and was defeated by the subtle ploy of his own teammate.

When Zhabotinsky mustered all of his strength in the jerk to defeat Vlasov, the crowd was stunned. The former champion was incensed. How could a fellow countryman stoop to such a deceitful, conniving scheme? "I was choked with tears," he later wrote. "I flung the silver medal through the window. . . . I had always revered the purity, the impartiality of contests of strength. That night, I understood that there is a kind of strength that has nothing to do with justice."[2]

Just as Vlasov was deceived, so often are we. Indeed, the world is full of treacherous people—double-dealing businessmen, counterfeiters, flimflam artists. That's why the Bible exhorts us to be vigilant and forever watchful.

Of course, we are wise to understand that there is one who is out to deceive us all, the devil himself. Jesus called him, "A liar, and the father of it [lies]" (John 8:44). When the apostle Paul wrote Timothy, he warned him against the snares of the devil. If Satan wearies of using his snares to entrap us, he will then use his subtlety to lull us into an easy-going complacency. Never underestimate the power and deceitfulness of the devil. He too has "a kind of strength that has nothing to do with justice."

Martin Luther, in his great hymn, "A Mighty Fortress Is Our God," wrote:

> For still our ancient foe
> Doth seek to work us woe—
> His craft and power are great,
> And armed with cruel hate,
> On earth is not his equal.

Since we cannot beat the devil in a fair fight, we need an advocate. We need someone who can stand with us in the battle for right. When David, a shepherd boy, was only a lad, he went up against the giant, Goliath, the champion of the Philistines. He rejected the armor that was offered him and the conventional weapons of that day. He knew that he could never be victorious over this military monster in his own strength. He said, "The LORD that delivered me out of the paw of the lion, and out of the paw of the bear, he will deliver me out of the hand of this Philistine. . . . The LORD saveth not with sword and spear: for the battle is the LORD's" (1 Sam. 17:37, 47).

The apostle John said, "Ye are of God, little children, and have overcome them; because greater is he that is in you, than he that is in the world" (1 John 4:4). As we yield to the presence, wisdom, and strength of the Lord, we shall neither be overcome by the devil's intensity nor bamboozled by his deceitfulness.

Never on Sunday
Eric Liddell

In the process of developing character, we form convictions, standards by which our integrity and honesty are measured. As we seek to live life on the highest plain, the whole of society seems intent upon challenging our quest for the best and tempting us to compromise. The pressure to yield to temptation often comes in those areas that are seemingly small and insignificant. Yet, if the tempter finds a crack in the dike of our will, he will send a flood tide of temptations designed to defeat us. The challenge is to stand firm and have convictions that are immovable.

Early in this century a young Scotsman, a preacher, in fact, showed the courage not to compromise his convictions, not even for Olympic glory. Eric Liddell was so fast he was nicknamed the "Flying Scot." Liddell's favorite sport was rugby, but he abandoned that and focused his attention on running. He was a bandy-legged runner with awkward movements and an unorthodox style. His forte was the 100 meters.

In 1923 he gained national attention in his homeland by dominating the sprints at the Amateur Athletic Association championships. He was the favored choice to represent Great Britain in the 100 meters in the 1924 Olympic Games in Paris, France. Liddell was convicted, however, by his religious beliefs that he should not participate in a sporting event on Sunday. He declined the opportunity to run the 100 meters because he heard that the heats were to be run on the Lord's day.[1]

In the 1981 film *Chariots of Fire,* Liddell is portrayed as a sincere Christian who discovers as he is boarding a ship for passage to France that the 100-meter race is scheduled for a Sunday. Although the basic facts in the movie are true to the historical record, Liddell was actually properly informed six months before the Olympics that the race would occur on a Sunday.[2]

Harold Abrahams, the son of a Lithuanian Jew who had emigrated to London, won the 100 meters in the 1924 games. In fact, Abrahams was victorious over two favorite American sprinters, Jackson Scholz and Charley Paddock. Abrahams, running faster than he had ever run before, tied an Olympic record with a time of 10.6 seconds.

Having chosen not to run the 100 meters, Liddell was prepared to run the 200 and 400 meters. Not only did the scrupulous Scotsman not run in the 100 meters on Sunday, he spent that particular Sunday preaching a sermon in a Scottish church in Paris. Eric's resolve not to run on Sunday was complicated by a rousing protest from many of his own countrymen who thought he was being less than sympathetic to the country's Olympic cause. However, no runner was ever more determined to win than E. H. Liddell. He was a mild-mannered individual, but once said, "I do not like to be beaten."[3]

In the 400-meter trial heat, Josef Imbach, a locksmith from Switzerland, broke the tape at the finish line in 48 seconds. Imbach's time shattered the Olympic record of 48.2 seconds that had been established at the Stockholm games in 1912. In the semifinal heat, Horatio Fitch of Chicago set another Olympic record for the 400 meters by crossing the finish line at 47.8 seconds.

For the final heat the six competitors were David Johnson of Canada, Guy Butler of England, Imbach, John Taylor of the New York Athletic Club, Fitch, and Liddell. When the gun was fired, Liddell took off like a rabbit as if he were running a short dash. At the halfway mark his record was a remarkable 22.2 seconds. He actually increased his pace over the last half of the race and defeated the silver medalist by eight-tenths of a second.

Liddell successfully set a new Olympic record with his time of 47.6 seconds. Within twenty-four hours the Olympic record for the 400-meter run had been broken three times. Liddell also won a bronze medal for his effort in the 200 meters.[4]

In *Chariots of Fire,* Abrahams and Liddell are given a great deal of retrospective fame six decades after the Paris Olympics. The film is an absorbing and unusual drama featuring the chemistry between the Scottish parson and the Jewish Cambridge student. For a brief moment in time, the Olympic Games brought two men together in a beautifully sentimental setting before their choices sent them on different paths and toward different destinies.[5]

Abrahams became a radio commentator for the British Broadcasting Company, a lawyer, and a writer. He died in London at the age of seventy-nine. Liddell returned to China, where he had been born, and rejoined his missionary parents. In China he fulfilled his life's calling by serving as a minister of the gospel. He died of a brain tumor in a Japanese World War II internment camp at the age of forty-three.[6]

In *Chariots of Fire,* Hollywood staged a scene whereby Jackson Scholz handed Liddell a note just prior to the running of the 400 meters. That was a fictionalized version to enhance the dramatic moment of the movie, but it was not without an element of truth. A note of encouragement was handed to Liddell by an unnamed fan, presumably a Christian. The handwritten note said, "He who honors me, I will honor."[7] This verse is based on 1 Samuel 2:30 and suggests that God's promises are conditional. When we refuse to compromise and stand firm in our God-given convictions, He will fulfill His promises and provide untold blessings.

The Bible focuses upon a few individuals who simply refused to compromise. Joseph refused to compromise his purity when Potiphar's wife attempted to seduce him. Daniel refused to defile his body with the rich food of the king when he was tempted. Shadrach, Meshach, and Abednego risked everything when they refused to compromise their allegiance to God. When Peter and John were commanded not to speak in the name of Jesus, they answered, "For we cannot but speak the things which we have seen and heard" (Acts 4:20).

Get some God-honoring convictions and stand on them. Remember, right is right if nobody's right, and wrong is wrong if everybody is wrong.

V

FIVE

The Final Race and Beginning Glory

Wilma Rudolph

On November 12, 1994, the Nashville, Tennessee, media sadly reported the death of a champion. Wilma Rudolph was dead at the age of fifty-four, a victim of brain cancer. Because of the character and quality of Wilma's life, she will forever be a legend in American and Olympic sports history.

Wilma rose from the dust and ashes of poverty and physical disability to achieve international status. In life she was an inspiration to multitudes. In death she has left a legacy of service and humanitarian works that challenge the very best within us.

Born on June 23, 1940, in Clarksville, Tennessee, Wilma was the twentieth of twenty-two children and the daughter of Eddie and Blanch Rudolph. Her early years were marked by sickness and disability. She was told that she would never walk. She was stricken with double pneumonia, scarlet fever, and then contracted a mild form of polio.

Paralytic Poliomyelitis—how well do I remember this scourge that swept through the nation like a rampaging physical malignancy in the late 1940s and early 1950s. In the United States most cases of this highly communicable disease were reported during the warmer months and seemed to occur mostly in children between four and fifteen years of age. Therefore, the summer months, traditionally a time of outdoor fun, became a season of dread. In 1952, polio's peak year, 57,879 cases were reported along with 3,145 deaths.

During that ominous summer when this crippling virus suddenly and clandestinely invaded the hamlets and cities of America, churches and community centers were closed to children. Parents would not dare bring their children to public places for fear such close contact would escalate the epidemic. The whole of life was paralyzed with apprehension and fear.

The extent of Wilma's polio was not the most severe, but it was another factor on the growing list of liabilities that would reduce her chances of ever walking again. Yet, even as a child, Wilma had an unconquerable, indomitable spirit.

Standing upright was her first goal. Gaining strength in her shrunken legs through daily massages performed by family members provided encouragement and desire. Walking that first step with a cumbersome brace fueled the hope of ultimate glory.

Finally, when Wilma was nine years old, she discarded her leg braces and walked with an orthopedic shoe. Over time she hastened her pace, and the walk became a jog, the jog became a run. By her eleventh birthday, Wilma was running and jumping with the best of them. She was the epitome of courage and determination.

When the greatest goal of most teenagers was to get a driver's license, Wilma was hitching her wagon to a higher star. In 1956 the greatest aspiration of hordes of high school students was being fulfilled by "dragging" the local drive-in restaurant on Saturday nights. In the same year, Wilma Rudolph achieved her higher goal, qualifying for the Olympics in Melbourne, Australia.

Although Wilma was eliminated in the initial round in her first quest for Olympic glory, she returned home to Tennessee where she starred on her high school basketball team. Her subsequent exploits with Tennessee State's fabled Tiger Belles (the women's track team) are now legendary.

In 1960, Rome, the Eternal City, was the site of the Olympic Games. Like Hannibal, the Carthaginian who attacked the Romans in 218 B.C. with ninety thousand foot soldiers, twelve thousand horsemen, and forty elephants, Wilma took Rome by storm. She won the 100- and 400-meter dashes and anchored the 4x100 meter relay team. Interestingly, Wilma combined with Tennessee State teammates Martha Hudson, Lucinda Williams, and Barbara Johnson to challenge for this event.

Wilma may have easily turned in the best American track performance ever in Rome. She prevented a shutout of the United States in the women's events. She became the first American woman to win three gold medals in track and field in one Olympics.

For her record-breaking Olympic successes, she was dubbed "a lightening bolt in spikes." After retiring from competition in 1962, Wilma represented the United States as a goodwill ambassador to French West Africa. During the early 1960s she was a co-host of a network radio show, a spokesperson for Minute Maid orange juice, and an administrative analyst for UCLA. Later she accepted executive roles with a Nashville bank, a Nashville hospital, and a baking company in Indianapolis. She coached at DePauw University in Greencastle, Indiana, and became a circuit lecturer. She also served as president of the Wilma Rudolph Foundation, devoted to teaching youngsters that they too could overcome obstacles.

The story of Wilma Rudolph is the record of a small country girl who attained worldwide fame. She was aware of the responsibility that accompanied stardom and was motivated to use her personality, time, and talents to the glory of God and the honor of womanhood.

The memorial service for this Olympic champion was held in Clarksville, Tennessee, at the First Baptist Church on Madison Street. The fifteen-hundred-seat auditorium was packed with family members, friends, and adoring fans. Hundreds of people stood outside the church. Many could not hold back their tears. The Reverend James Victor, pastor of the Mount Olive Missionary Baptist Church, delivered the soul-stirring eulogy.

At Wilma Rudolph's funeral the pastor's message was entitled "The Final Race and Beginning Glory." He declared, "In 1960, Wilma Rudolph overcame a number of obstacles in Rome, the queen city of Italy . . . and crossed the finish line at the Olympic Games to receive many accolades and awards. . . . But I'm here to tell you that on Saturday morning [the day of her death] she crossed the finish line of life and traded in gold medals for a golden crown. She traded in the applause of this world to hear the sweet melodic voice of my Lord say, 'Servant, servant, well done.' She has traded away the glitz and glamour of this world for the glories of heaven.

"One of these days, not only Wilma, but all the saints of God will be able to sing the words of the great spiritual:

> I got a crown, you got a crown,
> All God's children got a crown.

When I get to heaven
I'm gonna put on my crown,
And walk all over God's heaven.

"If you were to ask me, What does Wilma Rudolph—that lightening bolt in spikes—do in heaven?" And then I would probably say, "Sometimes she sings with the heavenly chorus. Sometimes she sits under the shade of the tree of life, by the river of life. Sometimes she watches the pearly gates swing wide to welcome another runner who has finished the race. And sometimes she runs down the main highways in heaven, just kicking up gold dust on the streets of glory."

We are all in a race. Therefore, the Bible says, "let us run with patience the race that is set before us, Looking unto Jesus the author and finisher of our faith" (Heb. 12:1b–2a). This race that we call life is no preliminary event. It is not a dress rehearsal. This life is the only opportunity that we have to fulfill God's purpose for our existence. We either keep our eyes on Christ, submit to His authority, and finish the race under His watchful eye, or we go off course onto some broad, crowded thoroughfare that leads to destruction. Choose the narrow path selected by Wilma Rudolph that leads to life everlasting.

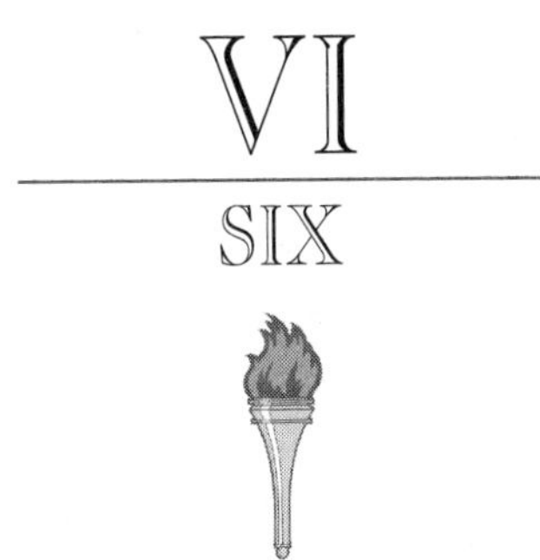

A Promise Keeper

Melvin Pender

Melvin Pender was motivated to succeed by a promise. When he was sixteen years old, he pledged to his mother, "I'm going to do something with my life to make you proud of me." Today Mel faces the prospects of an early retirement, and he looks back on a life overladen with accomplishments, enough to make any mother beam with pride.

Pender's fashionable ties and stylish wardrobe give the impression that he's under a modeling contract with *Gentleman's Quarterly,* but his workplace is in the notable CNN Center in downtown Atlanta. Every morning he goes to work in suite 405 in the south tower, the executive office complex of the Atlanta Hawks basketball team. This Atlanta native is in his sixth season as director of community affairs for the Hawks.

Tailor-made suits and offices with an atrium view have not always typified Mel's lot in life. There was a time when he wore army fatigues and lived on the often typhoon-targeted island of Okinawa.

Pender was stationed with the Eighty-second Airborne Division on this island off the southern coast of Japan and played football with a team called the Army Rangers. One day the coach said to the football team, "The Japanese are coming over from Osaka to compete against the Okinawans in a track meet. We have been invited to participate, and I want some of you men to contend for the trophy."

Because Mel was the fastest man on the football team, his involvement in the event was personally solicited. Although he protested that he had never run track and knew virtually nothing about the sport, he agreed to participate.

On the day of the event, an inspection delayed Pender's departure from the base. At last, having completed his responsibilities, he got away and hitchhiked to a place called Nargo, on the southern tip of the island. He arrived just in time for the meet. When his event was announced, he dug two holes in the ground. At the sound of the gun, Pender exploded out of his self-styled starting blocks and won his very first race in track.

There at twenty-four years of age, Mel Pender discovered he was a sprinter capable of superior velocity. For the first time he realized he had potential. Running would become the ingredient in life that would give him purpose and identity. He was beginning to make some deposits in his bank of promise to ensure that his mother would be proud of him. Pender was undefeated in twelve track meets in Okinawa.

In 1961 some of the troops were given seven days of rest and relaxation in Tokyo. It was then Pender learned that the burgeoning Japanese capitol was to be the host city for the 1964 Olympic Games. Inspired by what he had recently read about the former Olympic hero, Jesse Owens, Pender vowed to return to compete in the 1964 games.

A subsequent visit to Wilma Rudolph in Clarksville, Tennessee, fanned the flame of desire in Mel's heart to participate in the Tokyo games. The inspired sprinter reenlisted in the army but continued to pursue his dream. At a track meet in Washington, D.C., Pender soundly defeated some of the top sprinters in the nation. His ability to hurl himself into motion and his smooth acceleration were beginning to attract wide attention. The coach of the Pioneer Track Club in Philadelphia saw Pender in the Washington meet and invited him to join the prestigious Pennsylvania club.

While Mel was being widely accepted as an athlete, as an African American he was not always widely accepted as a person. Although desegregation legislation was being enacted, the American people discovered that old prejudices die hard.

After the track meet in Washington, Pender and a friend, a white distance runner named Chapelle from Fort Bragg, entered a restaurant. The proprietor welcomed Chapelle but refused to serve Pender. Of that experience, Mel exuded grace when he said, "I couldn't tell you how I felt when I walked into that restaurant wearing my country's military uniform to discover that I was not welcome. Something happened to me then. I realized that I needed to do something great with my life—something that not only would make my mother proud of me, but something that would give me self-respect and a sense of accomplishment. In fact, that experience drew me closer to God."

The restaurant experience convinced Pender to apply for officers candidate school. He was accepted and began the process of qualifying for commissioned officer status. While preparing to enhance his rank with the army, he was also preparing to enhance his chance to participate in the Tokyo Olympics. In 1962 he was sent to Fort Hood, Texas, to train with the army track team. It was at this point in Mel's career that Coach Jesse Lipscomb came into his life. Seeing Pender's potential, Coach Lipscomb drove him with relentless intensity. The daily grind included drills, exercises, calisthenics, weight training, a study of techniques, and running, running, running.

Mel was invited to the AAU championships in Saint Louis, a qualifying event for the Tokyo Olympics. In this event he outran some of the best sprinters in the world. This track meet provided an opportunity for Mel to meet Bob Hayes (who won the gold medal for the 100 meters in Tokyo), Henry Carr (who won the gold medal for the 200 meters in Tokyo), and O. Paul Drayton (who won the silver medal for the 200 meters in Tokyo). Pender was now officially qualified at age twenty-seven to represent the United States in the 1964 Olympic Games.

In the quarter finals in the 100 meters in Tokyo, Pender tore something loose in his rib cage. The attending physician in the infirmary confirmed that some muscles were torn and recommended bed rest, adding, "I don't think you'll be able to run in the semifinals."

Not only did Pender compete in the semifinals, but he led for the first 50 meters. He always managed to launch himself from the starting point with phenomenal speed. Armin Hary from Frankfurt, Germany, was often heralded for his "blitz start," but students of track-and-field events have often given Pender the edge. Some have justifiably recognized him as the fastest runner out of the starting blocks.

Despite torn muscles and running against the counsel of the physicians, Pender qualified for the finals. Once again his explosive start gave him the lead at the halfway mark. Suddenly a sharp pain pierced his side—the kind of pain that steals one's breath away and freezes men into motionless suspension. Pender, however, did not quit. He finished the race in sixth place out of eight runners. Unfortunately, he had to watch the remainder of the Olympic Games from the hospital.

The failed attempt to win a gold medal fueled Mel's desire to succeed. He completed his requirements for officers candidate school and graduated near the top of this class—another deposit in the bank of promise to make his mother proud.

Having conquered the challenge to become a commissioned officer, Pender began to look forward to the 1968 Olympic Games in Mexico City. A stint of duty in Vietnam did not deter his preparation. Pender sprinted up and down the roads in an army compound in South Vietnam, ever preparing himself for competition. The humidity was stifling. The temperature was oppressive. The presence of the enemy was ever threatening, but the desire to keep a promise, the passion to be the best and the dream of a gold medal would not die.

At last Pender was brought back to the United States where conditions were more conducive to Olympic training. The stateside itinerary prior to the 1968 games included Fort Sam Houston, Texas, and Fort MacArthur, California. It was during this time prior to the Mexico City games that Pender set world records in the 50-yard dash (5.0 seconds) and 70-yard dash (6.8 seconds), and tied the world record in the 60-yard dash (5.9 seconds). Several years later at the age of thirty-four, Pender broke the world's record in the 60-yard dash at 5.8 seconds.

At last the Atlanta native was sent to Tahoe on the California-Nevada border to join the other Olympic qualifiers for training at an altitude comparable to the elevation of Mexico City. Although the scenery was inviting and the facilities superior, an ominous cloud hung over the training complex. The unrest centered on the African-American athletes.

The assassination of Dr. Martin Luther King Jr. had a profound effect upon the entire nation. Robert Kennedy, who was making a strong bid for the presidency, had been gunned down a few days earlier. Many thought the deaths of these men would impede the progress that the country had been making toward racial justice.

Dr. Harry Edwards, an African-American sports sociologist from San Jose State College, had called for a boycott of the Olympic Games. He concluded that a boycott would serve to call attention to all the ways in which African Americans continued to suffer the indignities of second-class citizenship. Avery Brundage, president of the American Olympic Committee, fought to discourage the boycott. Some believed that his efforts to thwart the boycott were intimidating or at best suspect.

The African-American athletes who had trained so diligently and dreamed so passionately about the Olympics rejected the idea of the boycott. They did choose to protest racial injustice through a silent but graphic demonstration of support for their race.

Tommie Smith and John Carlos, the gold and bronze medal winners in the 200-meter dash in Mexico City, stood on the victory stand with heads bowed and black-gloved fists extended into the air. That highly visible but dignified gesture will forever remain the dominant image of those Olympic Games for most Americans.

John Carlos was Pender's roommate in Mexico City and gave him no prior notice of his intentions. Larry James and Ron Freeman swept the 400-meter finals and staged their own mild protest by wearing black berets and waving their ungloved fists at the crowd to and from the victory stand. Some of the American Olympians wore black armbands or black socks to show their solidarity.

Pender wore black shoes. He had asked Colonel Miller, who was representing the U.S. military at the games, for permission to do so. Pender explained, "The black athletes want to do something as a unit. It's nothing against America. I'm a soldier. I love my country. It's nothing against the flag. It's just something I have to do to show my support for my people."

The U.S. Olympic Committee promptly responded to the actions of Smith and Carlos by removing them from the Olympic team and the Olympic village. Some believe the committee's reaction was impulsive. America's black athletes had been under a tremendous amount of pressure. They were responding to a very difficult situation with a firm resolve clothed in respectability.[1]

In Mexico City, although Pender placed sixth once again in the 100 meters, he teamed with Charlie Green, Ronnie Ray Smith, and Ray Hines to win the 400-meter relay. Together they set a new world record of 38.23 seconds. Although Hines caught the Cuban anchorman, Enrique Figuerola, in the 400-meter relay to merit the gold for the U.S. team, Pender, who ran the second leg, was regarded as the fastest man that day. Perhaps it was all a matter of promises made and promises kept.

Since Mel's days of Olympic glory he has enjoyed a professional career with the International Track Association. In 1976 he earned a degree in social science from Adelphi University in Long Island, New York. In that same year he retired from the U.S. Army as a captain after twenty-one years of active duty. A commanding officer in the Eighty-second Airborne Division, he earned a bronze star for his service in Vietnam and served as the U.S. Military Academy's head track coach for six years. His accomplishments in the field of sports, business, civic concerns, and community relations are extensive and notable. For his innumerable successes, Mel Pender is careful to give God the glory. He acknowledges, "My explosive speed was a gift. I was born with it. I had a mission to run faster than any sprinter in the world, but I didn't do it alone."

Is Mel Pender a promise keeper? Yes, indeed. Because of his numerous accomplishments in the past, he has surely made his mother proud just as he promised. Today he continues to be a credit to his mother, his race, his nation, the world of sports, and the One who created him to run fast.

There is a movement today challenging men to be Promise Keepers. It is a needed emphasis because it seems no longer are many men as good as their word. Once there was a time when a man's word was his bond, but today promises seem to be given indiscreetly, lightly regarded, and seldom kept. However, the Bible says, "That which is gone out of thy lips thou shalt keep and perform" (Deut. 23:23). According to Holy Scripture, a promise to God is particularly binding. The writer of Ecclesiastes declares, "When thou vowest a vow unto God, defer not to pay it; for he hath no pleasure in fools: pay that which thou hast vowed. Better is it that thou shouldest not vow, than that thou shouldest vow and not pay" (Eccles. 5:4–5). Therefore, it is incumbent upon those who wish to be known for their character and integrity to keep their promises.

VII
SEVEN

A Father to the Finish
Derek Redmond

Not all Olympic gold medalists are worthy heroes; not all heroes are Olympic gold medalists. There are more ingredients in hero status than just winning, and sometimes the greatest heroes are found among those who tried but failed. The litmus test for a true hero is based on honor, courage, determination, and faith. Sometimes the character traits seen in an athlete who falters and fails in some heralded contest teaches us more than the athlete who wears "the gold."

Sociologists tell us that character traits are formed at an early age. Even in the process of teaching a child to walk, the attributes of a noble character can be instilled. Loving parents teach their tiny tots to walk by coaching each step, praising each success, and softening each fall. Parents who want to instill character in their children, however, not only teach them how to walk, but where to walk.

I think Derek Redmond, a twenty-eight-year-old British runner, must have had a father intent upon instilling character in his son. In the 1992 Summer Olympics, Derek was running in the semifinals of the 400 meters. He had disciplined himself and dedicated himself to a rigorous training routine for this monumental event. He had demonstrated his world-class speed for several years in numerous track events. Many of England's sports enthusiasts and interested observers from other countries thought Redmond had an excellent chance of winning a gold medal. *If not a gold medal, at least a silver one is within my grasp,* Redmond thought.

Running the race of his life, Derek rounded the first bend in the lead. His fluid motion was a picture of poise and grace. The fresh air that filled his lungs with every breath gave him an euphoric feeling. A sense of confidence enveloped him, for he knew that he had not yet tested the limits of his ability in this race. Suddenly he felt a sharp pain in the back of his leg. It was as if some malignant foe had shot an arrow through a beautiful balloon that was soaring to the heights. Derek fell to the track in agony, grabbing his torn hamstring.

Redmond waved off the approaching medical attendants and rose from the track. Hopelessly out of contention, he struggled forward to complete the race. He had competed in other track meets and had always raced to the finish line with a passion to excel. He was a crowd pleaser and had always enjoyed the adulation of the grandstands. He could have hobbled to the sidelines and done what would have been expected of most athletes under similar circumstances. However, when Redmond became limited physically, his true character surfaced. The determination that had brought him to Barcelona had purged the word *quit* from his vocabulary.

As Derek hopped down the final stretch, a rather large man in a T-shirt, khaki pants, and a ball cap emerged from the crowded grandstands. The middle-aged man brushed aside a security guard and rushed to Derek's side. The older man was Jim Redmond, the the injured runner's father.

"You don't have to do this," the father told his son. "You don't have to put yourself through this." However, the younger Redmond, grimacing, declared that it was his intention to finish this race because four years earlier in Seoul, Korea, he had encountered similar problems. In the 1988 Olympics Derek had dropped out of the 400-meter race ninety seconds before his first heat—hamstring problems. This time his unwavering resolve was to finish the race.

High atop Barcelona's Montjuïc, Derek Redmond, with the help of his father, fought toward the finish line. Arm in arm and shoulder to shoulder, they stayed in Derek's lane and persevered to the end. By the time they had reached the finish line the security guards had backed off. The other runners had turned to see this display of courage and fatherly love. Every eye in the crowd was riveted upon the dramatic scene. Practically every spectator was standing in awe of this tender moment in Olympic history. The applause was thunderous. Many wept.

Sports Illustrated captured the essence of the event with these words: "Derek didn't walk away with the gold medal, but he walked away with an incredible memory of a father who, when he saw his son in pain, left his seat in the stands to help him finish the race."

Let us be thankful for fathers who teach us to walk and inspire us to run, but who are also there to pick us up when we fall. Our heavenly Father is like that. When we falter and fail and are tempted to give up on our dreams, He wants us to know He is with us all the way to the finish line.

"Even the youths shall faint and be weary, and the young men shall utterly fall: But they that wait upon the LORD shall renew their strength; they shall mount up with wings as eagles; they shall run, and not be weary; and they shall walk, and not faint" (Isa. 40:30–31).

The Platform of Honor

Gail Devers

The platform of honor is where the Olympic athletes receive their medals of gold, silver, and bronze. Traditionally, platforms are used to provide visibility to those who are worthy of recognition and respect. The pathway to the Olympic platform of honor is often marked by pain, hardship, and difficulty. There is no shortcut to this podium of recognition, no easy street to Olympic success. In the march to Olympic glory there is no gain without pain.

The history of the Olympic Games provides a myriad of stories about athletes who have overcome trials, tests, and even tragedy to get to the winner's platform. Every athlete who earns the privilege of standing on the platform has his own story of personal triumph. Yet every Olympian, regardless of which country he represents and irrespective of how well or how poorly he does in his chosen event, has accomplished much in winning the right to participate. In every Olympiad an impressive array of athletes, through determination and perseverance, fight their way to the platform of honor. There they stand for their moment of glory to bask in the sunlight of adulation and recognition.

Once under entirely different circumstances I found myself on a rather interesting platform in Houston, Texas. I was attending my very first Southern Baptist Convention in June 1968. While there, I realized that Dr. Billy Graham was going to be speaking at the closing convention session. So on that last day I rearranged my flight schedule to remain in the city and hear Dr. Graham. Arriving at the Music Hall where the convention sessions were being held, I discovered that the huge arena had already been filled to capacity and that the fire marshals would not permit anyone else to enter the building. I began to walk around the Music Hall in hopes of finding some door, some window, some service entrance whereby I could gain access to this final convention session. Two circuits around the Music Hall availed nothing, and my hopes of hearing Dr. Graham were beginning to wane.

I decided to make one last effort to enter the convention complex by walking around the building once more. As I approached the back of the hall, several cars pulled up to a restricted parking area. I was close enough to recognize that Billy Graham and George Beverly Shea were in the first car. Several other well-dressed, dignified men got out of the other two cars and started toward the back entrance. Should I dare fall in step with these men in hopes of achieving my goal? Was this God's provision for my problem?

I turned to join this impressive entourage step for step. I was confidently bringing up the rear as we walked through the door. Since I was in Dr. Graham's company, no one ventured to ask for my credentials. As we walked down a long corridor, the security officials nodded approvingly as our group passed by. I reciprocated with smiles and even an occasional handshake. We walked up some steps, through a curtain, up a ramp, up another short flight of steps, and there I stood on the platform at the Music Hall before thousands of people with the Billy Graham team. I presumed that Dr. Graham concluded that I had accompanied them as a representative of the convention. I'm quite sure that the convention officers somehow must have thought that I was associated with Dr. Graham's organization. The truth is that I was able to remain on the platform of honor not twenty feet away from Dr. Graham until the benediction was pronounced.

That was 1968, the year the Olympics were held in Mexico City. My ascendancy to the platform of honor was not in the Estadio Olimpico in Mexico City, but in the Music Hall in Houston, Texas. My position on the platform was not the result of hard work, but a combination of audacity and good fortune. I did not receive a gold medal, nor did I hear "The Star-Spangled Banner" played in recognition of my achievement. But with a bit of ingenuity and determination I was able to turn a problem into a pearl. A rather hopeless situation was transformed into an unforgettable experience.

Gail Devers has a story of her own that is powerful and compelling. She got to the platform of honor through a path of pain and perseverance. In 1988 this speedster from Palmdale, California, set an Olympic record in the 100-meter hurdles but then fell victim to an inexplicable illness. Her symptoms included migraine headaches, temporary loss of vision in one eye, sudden fluctuation in weight, involuntary shaking and convulsions, amnesia spells, hair loss, frequent menstrual cycles, and supersensitive skin that would bleed from the slightest scrape or scratch.[1]

For two years doctors vainly attempted to diagnose Devers's puzzling ailment. Her symptoms were attributed to diabetes, exhaustion, and tension before she was at last diagnosed with Graves disease. The disease is only detected by using laboratory tests that measure the levels of thyroid hormones in the serum, or by determining the ability of the thyroid gland to take up radioactive iodine.[2]

This hyperthyroid condition can be treated successfully with a medication that is a beta-blocker. Unfortunately, this drug is banned by the Olympic committee, and Devers refused to take it. She chose to submit herself to radiation therapy to help resolve her illness. But the side effects of these treatments negatively affected other body tissues. She came within forty-eight hours of having both feet amputated before her radiation therapy was regulated.[3]

Within several weeks Devers was gingerly walking around the track at UCLA. That was the first step back toward the competitive circuit after a two-year hiatus. Within a few more weeks, Devers's coach, Bob Kersee, had her running and hurdling with astounding results. In the summer of 1991 Gail won the Athletic Congress 100-meter hurdles. Later she won the silver medal in the 100-meter hurdles in the Tokyo World Championships. Kersee had confidence that Devers could succeed in the 100-meter sprint. When it came time to qualify for the 1992 Barcelona games, she made the Olympic team in both the hurdles and the 100-meter dash.[4]

When Gail marched into Barcelona's Olympic stadium for the opening ceremonies, she felt prepared mentally and physically for the challenges ahead. She became the world's fastest woman by winning the 100 meters, although it was by the narrowest of margins. She beat Juliet Cuthbert of Jamaica by one-hundredth of a second.

A few days later, Devers was headed for her second gold medal by holding a commanding lead in the 100-meter hurdles. However, her pace was so fast that she reached the last hurdle earlier than expected and smashed against it with her forward foot. Gail fell headlong onto the track but crawled across the finish line in fifth place.

The sixty-five thousand spectators high atop Barcelona's Montjuïc witnessed Devers's fall with empathetic eyes. Some of the spectators knew full well the difficult pathway Gail had taken to get to the Olympic Games. Her winsome spirit had already captivated many in the audience, and they too felt the hurt and disappointment that she had to experience in her fall. However, Gail was dismayed only momentarily. She picked herself up, smiled, and nodded responsively to the crowd.

Gail, a PK (preacher's kid), had never forgotten the lessons she had been taught in the home of her Christian parents. In her own heart she knew that the important thing is not whether you win or lose, but how you run the race. After all, she had already found her way to the platform in the 100-meter race. She already had one gold medal draped around her neck, even if it took two years to produce it.

In the march to Olympic glory and in the march of Christian soldiers, there is no gain without pain and there is no crown without a cross. In fact, Jesus Christ did not suffer and die to save us from suffering but that our suffering might be like His. It is through suffering that life's greatest lessons are learned and God's greatest miracles are discovered.

In Job of the Old Testament we see the portrait of a man who maintained his devotion to God in the midst of untold suffering and loss. His herds and flocks were either stolen or destroyed. His servants were slain. His sons and daughters died in a tornado. Job was then afflicted with boils that covered his body. In all of his adversity, however, Job maintained his integrity and his faith in God. In fact, Job said, "Naked came I out of my mother's womb, and naked shall I return thither: the LORD gave, and the LORD hath taken away; blessed be the name of the LORD. In all this Job sinned not, nor charged God foolishly" (Job 1:21–22).

In the last chapter of the Book of Job we discover that his steadfast commitment to God was justly rewarded. The Bible says, "the LORD gave Job twice as much as he had before . . . [and] blessed the latter end of Job more than his beginning" (Job 42:10b, 12a).

Anyone can serve God when the sun is shining and everything is coming up roses. However, the person who honors God in the most difficult circumstances and in the midst of great suffering will be justly rewarded and will one day be able to stand on God's platform of honor.

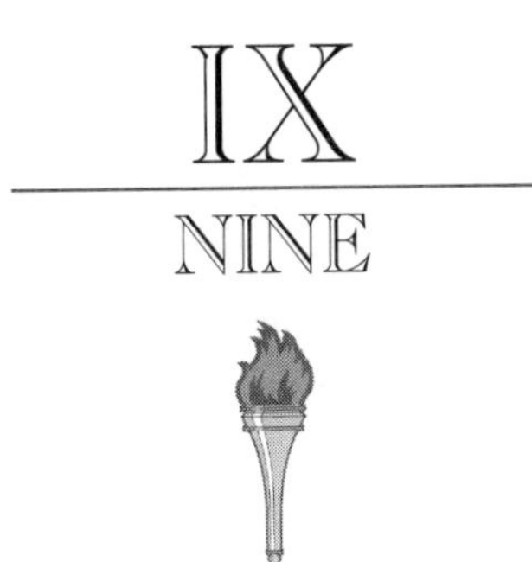

IX NINE

Practice Makes Perfect—Almost

Károly Takács

I am not a concert pianist. Perhaps I could never have been one. I will never know because I never practiced. I pretended to practice, but it was a poor imitation of the real thing, just enough to fool my mother. Concert pianists are known for their discipline and their devotion to practicing.

Károly Takács was not a pianist, but he proved that practice makes perfect—well, almost. Takács was a sharpshooter who is among the most deserving of all the Olympic gold medalists in history.

Károly Takács was born in 1909 and grew up in Budapest, Hungary. As a young man he was conscripted into military service. The Hungarian army provided the perfect environment for him to sharpen his skills as a marksman. His long hours of hard work, his steady hand

and eagle-eye precision in handgun practice sessions soon attracted the attention of his superiors.

The remarkable skill Takács demonstrated with a pistol merited him an early promotion to the rank of sergeant. He was assigned the responsibility of instructing recruits in the use of handguns. He delighted to teach the techniques of good marksmanship. This unique instructional role also afforded him the ability to practice his art and hone his competitive skills. He was continually throwing down the gauntlet, challenging his fellow soldiers to match his performance in marksmanship.

By the late 1930s Takács was known as the European pistol champion of the decade. He was a member of the Hungarian World Championship Pistol Shooting Team in 1938 when tragedy struck. While serving in the Hungarian army, a grenade exploded in his right hand—his pistol hand—and shattered it completely. An amputation was necessary.[1]

When Takács awoke in the hospital and realized that his right hand—the hand that had made him a superior marksman—had been amputated, he was devastated. So often those who lose a limb experience not only physical pain but psychological and emotional pain as well.

Upon leaving the hospital, Takács went into almost complete seclusion. He was a proud man, and his family and friends wondered if he could accept his ill-fated lot. His choice to isolate himself and reluctance to communicate precipitated even greater concern. Some concluded that he was in a state of denial and simply unwilling to accept his tragic misfortune. Others reasoned that the accident had brought on a deep depression that prompted these seasons of withdrawal.

He had dreamed of participating in the 1940 Olympic Games. Knowledgeable people from almost every country in Europe considered him one of the strongest contenders for the gold medal. World War II, however, necessitated the cancellation of the Olympic Games in 1940 and 1944. Yet the war was something of an ally to Takács. While this great global conflict wreaked havoc across the world, it gave Takács time to collect his thoughts, heal emotionally, and reestablish his life's goals.

One day early in Takács's recovery process he unexpectedly bolted from his bedroom with a pistol in his hand. When his wife saw him with his handgun, she wondered if he might take his own life. Without saying a word, he disappeared out the back door of their cottage. She began to plead with him not to leave her. Standing on the threshold of the back door she was frozen with fear as she saw him disappear into the woods behind their house.

Suddenly a shot was fired. As it echoed through the woods she was gripped with a horrible thought, that Károly had done what she feared most. She slumped helplessly to the floor, writhing in agony. Suddenly she heard another shot ring through the air, and another, and another.

With the adrenaline surging through her body, she rose to her feet to investigate. With her heart beating like a triphammer and her mind ablaze with wonder, fear, and confusion, she rushed into the woods and found her husband with a bandaged, handless right arm behind him. With the pistol in his faltering left hand, Károly aimed at a target in the distance. His fading depression had given way to a rising determination. Like the proverbial phoenix rising from its ashes, Takács had begun the journey back to his coveted status as a superior marksman.

The days of practice wore into weeks and then months and years. Undaunted, Takács taught himself to shoot with his left hand. Ten years later, as he neared his thirty-ninth birthday, he stood atop the highest platform at the 1948

Brisley Olympic Games in London as the winner of the gold medal. The band played the Hungarian national anthem, and the crowd roared its approval, for the people realized that the first-place medal had been won at a great cost.

At the Olympic Games in 1952 in Helsinki, Finland, Takács won the silhouette shooting championship for a second time. The second gold medal marked him as one of only five competitors to have defended an Olympic shooting title successfully. Takács finished the second day with sixty hits and a point total of 579—one ahead of Szilard Kun, also of Hungary. The bronze medalist in 1952 was George Lichiardol of Rumania. There was a field of fifty-three competitors in this marksmanship event. Takács was not perfect, but almost. It was enough for the gold, a gold medal won once again by the determination to overcome seemingly insurmountable odds.

I think perhaps the apostle Paul was thinking about the ancient Olympic Games when he wrote in 1 Corinthians 9:24–25: "Know ye not that they which run in a race run all, but one receiveth the prize? So run, that ye may obtain. And every man that striveth for the mastery is temperate in all things. Now they do it to obtain a corruptible crown; but we an incorruptible." If the effort, the determination, and the desire demonstrated by Károly Takács in his successful quest to win two gold medals was translated into the spiritual realm—if we would only use that kind of discipline to serve the Lord—what a remarkable difference it would make in the Christian enterprise. What a remarkable difference it would make in our lives individually!

Clean Living
Fred Alderman

When I heard that Fred Alderman was the oldest gold medalist living in Georgia, I decided to pay him a visit. On a sultry, overcast Friday morning in August, I turned my automobile toward one of Georgia's quaint little towns—Social Circle. This charming hamlet, founded in 1836, consisting of three thousand inhabitants is about forty-five miles from Atlanta.

Driving into town, I headed for The Mews, a retirement center and nursing home. Inquiring as to the whereabouts of Fred Alderman, I was directed to a row of apartments where the more self-sufficient residents lived. When I knocked on the door, Alderman opened it with a scowl on his face and said, "I didn't expect you this early, but since you're here, come on in."

Admittedly, it was a rather inauspicious beginning. I entered the apartment with some fear and trepidation, but within a matter of minutes his scowl turned into a smile. As we began to talk about his exploits on the track, his eyes brightened and the day turned out to be one of the most delightful experiences of my life. I found my host to be chronologically gifted (he was more than ninety years old), fit as a fiddle, and blessed with total recall. Alderman has subscribed to the *Track and Field* magazine forever, reads it with devotion, and may know more about the Olympics than any living person.

One of the eye-catchers in the apartment was a large framed poster of a runner with a caption that read: IX OLYMPIAD—AMSTERDAM 1928. Beside the poster were two medals perfectly positioned in a bronze frame. The black felt background enhanced the medals visually and seemed to give added significance to them. The first medal was earned by Alderman during the 1928 games. The second medal was the genuine article—the prized and coveted trophy of Olympic heroes.

My new friend took the framed medals off the wall and handed them to me. I was surprised at their size. They were larger than I had expected. Having studied the games intensely for more than a year, I felt a wave of Olympic history sweeping over my soul. As I held the medals in my hand, I recalled the victories of Paavo Nurmi, Jesse Owens, Sonja Henie, George Foreman, Al Oerter, Mark Spitz, Bruce Jenner, Nadia Comaneci, Eric Heiden, Carl Lewis, and scores of others. The tradition, the train of victors, the discipline and commitment represented by those medals overwhelmed me.

On the coffee table was a wooden shoe, which I also took to be a token from the 1928 games in Amsterdam. Beside it was a small, worn diary containing some of Alderman's personal impressions of the trip to the Netherlands and Europe, along with the autographs of many of the 1928 Olympians: Ray Barbuti, George Baird, Bud Spencer, Jackson Scholz, Charlie Paddock, and Loren Murchison.

I discovered that my host for the day had been born in Orleans, Michigan, on June 24, 1905. Fred and his brother, A. L., who was thirteen years his senior, grew up with a fascination for running. Even as small lads they both seemed to enjoy seeing just how fast their legs would carry them. The family farm was almost a mile from the train depot in Orleans. When Fred heard the whistle from an approaching train as it rounded a bend four miles away, he would accept the challenge of trying to beat the train to the station. Across the pastureland he would run into town to meet the locomotive and invariably was there to greet it when it chugged into the station.

A. L. went to Michigan State to exhibit his athletic abilities in running track. He had already demonstrated his giftedness in this area by stealing the show at the county track meet. Fred's older brother won the 100, 220, 440, the broad jump, and the pole vault at the meet. At Michigan State, A. L. took the school by storm in his first year by setting a freshman record in the 100-yard dash at 10.1 seconds.

That record stood as a towering testimony of A. L.'s speed for twelve long years. It was broken by younger brother Fred during his freshman year at the university in East Lansing. Fred's time was 10 seconds flat.

The freshman event was just the beginning of a sparkling collegiate career for the younger Alderman. At Michigan State, Fred had rolled up victory after victory in the 100-yard dash, the 220-yard dash, and multiple victories as a part of the one-half-mile relay team. Grantland Rice, America's most noted sports announcer in those days, counted Michigan State's 1927 one-half-mile relay team as the best in the nation. In the same year that Babe Ruth was establishing a new home run record in Yankee Stadium, the Michigan State track team was ringing up victories on campuses all over the Midwest.

One of Alderman's happiest college memories was Michigan State's defeat of Notre Dame. The rivalry between the two schools was intense. Knute Rockne, Notre Dame's football coach, and Ralph Young, the football and track coach at Michigan State, were good friends and had established a tradition of dual track meets involving the two schools. Michigan State had never beaten the Fighting Irish, but the Spartans' hopes were riding high for the 1927 meet. Alderman had won the 100, 220, and the broad jump in this dual meet. They were down to the last event and needed to place second in the javelin to win the contest. Fred had performed well in this event in the past, but the present challenge required a throw that would outdistance the effort of Jack Elder. Elder was an All-American halfback for Notre Dame and a strong, powerful athlete.

Coach Young walked over to Fred and said, "Alderman, this is it. If you beat Elder and capture second place, we will go home in victory." I won't tell you who won, but I did see the headlines of the newspaper that heralded that momentous event. In bold letters it simply read: MICHIGAN STATE SURPRISES IRISH WITH TRACK WIN.

Fred permitted me to rummage through a box of newspaper clippings. Some of the articles were more than seventy years old. They were worn, faded, and tattered, but they marvelously captured the sporting accomplishments of Alderman's past. One article referred to him as "Michigan State's lithe toast." Another heralded him as "the greatest sprinter turned out in the middle west in years." One newspaper had a picture of Alderman winning the intercollegiate 100-yard dash in 1927 at Soldier Field in Chicago. At the same meet he set a new collegiate record in the 220 at 21.1 seconds.

The Social Circle resident declared that if the Olympic Games had been held in 1927, he would have been in the 100 meters and the 200 meters. However, the games were in 1928, and he qualified to participate in the 1,600-meter relay. The qualifying events were held in Boston and Philadelphia. Several days after the tryouts the American athletes who had qualified for the games boarded the great ship, *President Roosevelt,* for the trip to Amsterdam. The journey across the Atlantic took nine days. Alderman said, "Between the three or four training days lost prior to our departure and the nine days aboard the ship, we all basically arrived in Amsterdam in less than top physical condition."

On board the *President Roosevelt,* the Olympians were able to do some running in place, some calisthenics, and a few exercises. They were unable to do anything, however, to maintain the level of fitness necessary for Olympic competition. Once in the Netherlands there was no Olympic village to accommodate the athletes as has become customary in more recent years. The American team had to remain on board the ship. The circumstances were certainly not conducive to performing at one's best.

The events for the sprinters were scheduled during the first days of the games, and the American runners were dominated by their competitors. Alderman said, "I'd never seen anything like it. Our athletes looked like they were running uphill. Our 100-meter men who had run 10.6 in the Olympic trials in Boston got beat with a 10.8 time in Amsterdam."

Consequently, the U.S. team performed poorly in the track-and-field events. Jackson Scholz, for example, was America's great hope in the 200 meters. In the tryouts in Boston he broke the world's record in the 200 meters, but in Amsterdam he was a full second slower than in the tryouts. Alderman said, "I couldn't believe our sprinters were that bad, but they were."

The only three track events won by the U.S. team that year were the 400-meters and the two relays. Ray Barbuti, a former captain of the Syracuse University football team, won the 400 meters. The U.S. team of Frank Wykoff, James Quinn, Charles Borah, and Henry Russell won the 400-meter relay. Alderman's team, including George Baird, Emerson "Bud" Spencer, and Barbuti, won the 1,600-meter relay and set a new world record in the process.

In the interview I had built up our conversation to ask my most pertinent, passionate question of the day: "Mr. Alderman, how did you feel when you received your medal and heard our national anthem played by the Olympic band?" I waited for the emotion-filled answer with joyful anticipation.

"Oh," Alderman replied, "I was sick to my stomach. That's why I hated to run the 400 meters. I ran the 200 meters and never had a problem. But if I had to run the quarter, it nearly always made me throw up."

After the Olympic Games in Amsterdam, Alderman joined some of the other American athletes and went to Cologne, Germany, to run in a 400-meter relay, set a world record, and win the largest medal of his life. A week after the event in Cologne he ran a 220 in London. So, ultimately, he ran three different distances on his Olympic trip. Fred Alderman took advantage of his "one moment in time."

The "lithe toast of Michigan State" still weighs approximately the same 136 pounds that he weighed when he ran in the Amsterdam games. He has remained close to the track-and-field scene for more than seventy years. For thirty-three of those years he served as the starter for track meets at Georgia Tech. "It's a very important job," he declares. "Not everyone knows just when to say, 'Take your mark! get set!' and fire the gun. I was one of the best." Fred Alderman left me with the impression that he could easily be the best at just about anything he chose to do in life.

While visiting with my new friend, he opened a letter from Coca-Cola, one of the sponsors of the 1996 games, informing him that he had been selected as a semifinalist in another Olympic contest. The winners will have their portraits added to a fifteen-story mural to be painted on the Carter Residential Hall near the Olympic Stadium in Atlanta.

As we came near the conclusion of the interview, I asked, "To what do you attribute your long life?"

"Clean living," he answered. "I have eaten right, exercised regularly, and avoided bad habits. When I could no longer engage in vigorous exercise, I started dancing. Square dancing helped keep me in shape. I liked it. I was a good dancer. I could move pretty fast."

As I thanked Fred Alderman for his time and stood to depart, he insisted on walking me to my car. As we walked together I said, "Mr. Alderman, you're a nice looking man."

He smiled and said, "You are, too." But then he sort of gave me a back hand to the midsection as he continued, "but you need to get rid of that."

It was a terse reminder that a little body maintenance probably would not hurt me. I remembered Paul's words to the believers in Corinth: "What? know ye not that your body is the temple of the Holy Ghost which is in you, which ye have of God, and ye are not your own? For ye are bought with a price: therefore glorify God in your body, and in your spirit, which are God's" (1 Cor. 6:19–20).

Every human being is given one body as an entrustment from God. The body is neither to be misused or abused but nurtured and cared for. Some abuse their bodies through drugs and alcohol. Others misuse their bodies because they do not understand that the only form of safe sex outside the bond of marriage is abstinence. Still others refuse to honor the needs of their bodies through neglect. Some people neglect their bodies by not getting sufficient rest. Others neglect their bodies by not eating the right foods. Perhaps even more people neglect their bodies by failing to exercise properly. The believer's body is the vehicle through which God's spirit dwells and through which God's spirit moves to accomplish His work in our world today. Therefore, the body must be maintained with meticulous care.

Exercise! One! Two! Three! Four!

One Way Out of a Traffic Jam

Kip Keino

Almost everyone has been trapped in the snarl of heavy traffic. Sometimes the freeways of Atlanta more nearly resemble a parking lot than a thoroughfare. The true character of most motorists will begin to surface in a prolonged traffic jam. Some motorists allow their blood to boil, and their emotional equilibrium tilts on the side of uncontrolled indignation. Others display the patience of Job, even in the midst of the most congested conditions.

Some people have learned to use traffic jams to their advantage. They use mobile telephones to return calls. They dictate messages on their microcassette recorders. They mentally prepare for upcoming appointments and responsibilities. If there's no way to escape the snarl of a traffic jam, perhaps there are some ways you can find to redeem the time when you are hemmed in by cars and trucks on every side.

H. Kipchoge "Kip" Keino got caught in a traffic jam in Mexico City on October 20, 1968. He was on his way to Estadio Olympico to participate in another event in the Nineteenth Olympiad. Kip was trapped in a traffic jam, but he found a way out of his dilemma.

Estadio Olympico, an impressive athletic arena, was the site of the opening and closing ceremonies and the track-and-field events for the 1968 games. This massive architectural masterpiece is a sunken stadium across the street from the National University of Mexico.

Kip Keino of Kenya was being transported to this colossal coliseum to represent his country in the 1,500 meter race. Mexico City's public transportation system was being taxed to the limit, and private citizens with cars anxiously volunteered to provide supplemental transportation to the visitors. The streets were overcrowded, and the traffic was moving at a snail's pace. Kip tried to be patient but observed that the pedestrians were moving at a faster pace than the car in which he was traveling. When it became apparent that he could be late for his event, Keino thanked his chauffeur for the ride, got out of the automobile, and jogged the last mile to the stadium.

Kip was not about to be deterred by a traffic jam. In fact, this kinetic Kenyan has always been the quintessential problem solver. Throughout his life, Kip has not seen difficult circumstances as oppressive problems, but as opportunities to trust God. So Keino abandoned his vehicle of transportation and headed for the stadium on foot—running.[1]

After having run the rest of the route to the stadium while his competitors were resting and preparing themselves mentally for the race, Keino not only won the gold medal in the 1,500 meters, but achieved what was considered impossible. His time of 3 minutes 34.9 seconds broke the Olympic record made at sea level by the swift Herb Elliott of Australia eight years earlier at the games in Rome. Kip, sporting wide two-inch sideburns level with his mouth and a thin mustache, smiled as he mounted the victory platform.

Not only was Keino disadvantaged by having run to the stadium, but he was suffering a gall bladder infection that required surgery shortly after the games. Additionally, Kip had expended much of his stamina in two earlier Olympic events—the 5,000 and the 10,000 meters.

The longer race was first, and Keino was running with the leaders near the end of the race when he doubled up in pain and fell down. Although he was disqualified for veering off the track and falling in the infield, he got up and finished the race. Four days later Kip finished second in the 5,000 meters to Mohamed Gammoudi of Tunisia who won by four feet.

In winning the 1,500 meters, Keino had to beat the great recordholder, Jim Ryun of the United States. Ryun had beaten Keino at sea level a year earlier with a sizzling race of 3 minutes 33.1 seconds. In fact, Keino had never defeated Ryun, so the challenge was clear and bold. Keino's fellow countryman, Ben Jipcho, served as his rabbit and set the pace early in the race. Then, in the second lap, Keino sprinted wide and came up on Jipcho as Ryun settled into ninth place. Ryun was well known for his ability to accelerate and "kick" into high gear down the stretch.

However, Kip's intention was clear: spread so much red Tartan track between himself and Ryun that a recovery would be impossible. At forty yards back Ryun turned on the "jets," but there was too much ground to make up in the rarefied air of Mexico City. Furthermore, Keino had too much left. He won a spectacular race, the fastest 1,500 meters ever run at such an altitude. Kip, who was more accustomed to running at higher altitudes, had even improved his personal record by 1.2 seconds. This notable accomplishment was not bad for a man who had survived an exhausting week, who was battling a gall bladder infection, and who had had to overcome a traffic jam by jogging to the stadium.

While Kip was laboring to win the 1,500 meters, his wife, Phyllis, was in labor back in Kenya, giving birth to their third daughter. She was born on the day of Keino's great victory and named Milka Olympia in honor of her father's triumph in Mexico City.

Today the Keinos live on their Kazi Mingi farm in Kenya's western highlands. Kip is still actively involved in turning problems into opportunities. Throughout their marriage, Kip and Phyllis have been rescuing children from dilemmas far worse than traffic jams.

While on patrol as a law enforcement officer in northern Kenya in the mid-1960s (before the Mexico City games), Keino found three children wandering without parents. He and Phyllis, a nurse, took them into their home at the police academy. The children were starving to death. "They were eating soil," Kip said. The Keinos fed them, clothed them, and provided for their education. The Kazi Mingi farm has since become a haven for starving and needy children. For the past thirty years the Keinos have provided a home for more than one hundred destitute children.[2]

The Keinos' project of caring for orphans is sometimes more exhausting and taxing than Kip's well-documented exploits at the 1968 Olympic Games, but they continue their ministry. Kip says, "Sometimes we get donations. But when we have no money, we just work harder." Kip Keino, a strong Christian, believes the adage recorded in the Bible in James 1:27: "Pure religion and undefiled before God and the Father is this, to visit the fatherless and widows in their affliction, and to keep himself unspotted from the world."

The Bible clearly teaches that pure religion is based on a personal faith in Jesus Christ. Once that faith is established, it will express itself in good works. The apostle Paul says, "For by grace are ye saved through faith; and that not of yourselves: it is the gift of God." But then he says, "we are his workmanship, created in Christ Jesus unto good works" (Eph. 2:8, 10). We cannot work our way to the cross. But once we have experienced the grace of the cross of Christ, we will demonstrate the reality of our Christianity by serving others. Like Kip Keino, you will want to rescue a hurting humanity from the traffic jams of life.

XII
TWELVE

Tearing Down the Walls
Olga Korbut

By the time I got to Moscow the Iron Curtain had been torn down. There never was a literal curtain of iron, not really. The Iron Curtain was a term used to describe the ideological barriers that had been erected by the Soviet Union between its satellites and the Western world. While the curtain may not have had tangible properties, it was a frightening reality. Sometimes philosophical walls, political walls, categorical walls are the most impenetrable and the most confining.

What the people of Russia endured under communist rule was baffling to the Western world. In 1938 Winston Churchill commented that the Soviet Union "is a riddle wrapped in a mystery inside an enigma."[1] One thing was certain, however: the USSR was an intimidating military power that seemed to hold the rest of the world at bay with its menacing scowl and bullying threats. Nikita Khruschev's warning from 1959, "We will bury you!" are words that still ring in the ears of many Americans.

So, for many years a great barrier stood between the Soviet Union and the free world. The cold war that prevailed was like an ominous cloud over the whole of civilization. When skirmishes and wars were not being fought, rumors of war abounded. The whole earth was a tension-filled globe suspended in insecurity.

Glasnost began to lessen some of the tensions between the communists and the Western world. In 1990 Mikhil Gorbachev saw the downward spiral of the Soviet economy and concluded that dramatic changes were needed in the Soviet system of government. He shifted his philosophical position and became a tenacious advocate of a multi-party political system. Consequently, the constitutional provision guaranteeing a monopoly of power for the Communist Party was eliminated. Under Premier Boris Yeltsin, the Iron Curtain has become mostly a grievous memory.

I was in the city of Kiev in the Ukraine on November 7, 1992, the anniversary of the establishment of the Russian Soviet Republic. Vladimir Ilyich Lenin became the head of the new government on that day in 1917. In Kiev a number of hard-core socialists had come together to place flowers at Lenin's statue in the heart of the city to commemorate the seventy-fifth anniversary of the communist takeover.

As I stood there on that cold, rainy, overcast day, I realized that only remnants of the Iron Curtain remained, but the devastation left in the wake of the long years of communist rule was clearly evident. Of all the emptiness I encountered in the Commonwealth of Independent States, however, the hearts of the people were the most empty of all. The communist propaganda and the suppression of thought created a void that all the teachings of Marx could never fill.

Given the restrictions placed upon the propagation of Christianity in the public schools of America, I was amazed that I had the privilege of speaking in the public schools of the Ukraine. I asked, "Is there a subject you would like me to address when I speak to the students and the faculty?"

The superintendent's reply was, "Why don't you tell them about your God and your view of creation. We'd like to hear about that, especially since we've heard nothing in our schools but atheistic evolution for three-fourths of the century."

During that unforgettable week, and on numerous occasions since my visit to the former Soviet Union, I have expressed my thanks to God for the hunger and openness of the people. The hearts of most were empty, but they wanted them filled with truth and significance. There is nothing with greater potential than an empty mind and heart. Since there is as much potential for evil as good in the human soul, the truth must be communicated.

When did all of the openness and receptivity of the people begin to surface? When did the Iron Curtain begin to fall? When did the Soviets begin to soften their propaganda? When did the attitude of the West toward the Soviet government begin to relax? Did the emergence of *glasnost* bring about the change? Was it the reforms of Gorbachev? Was it some kind of diplomatic détente? Did it begin with some kind of peace treaty?

Some think it all started in the 1972 Olympics when Olga Korbut dominated the center stage in the gymnastic events. After an impressive performance in the Twentieth Olympiad in Munich, Olga visited the United States. She went to the White House and encountered a man who commented on her diminutive statue. When he said, "You're so tiny," she responded by saying, "You're so big."[2] She thought the man was a reporter but soon discovered that he was none other than the president of the United States, Richard Nixon. Olga made a profound impression upon the president and the American people as well. After her visit, a Soviet foreign minister told her that she had done more to improve relations between the two countries than all the diplomats had accomplished in five years.

This little pixie elf from the Soviet Socialist Republic of Belorussia became the undisputed darling of the 1972 Olympics. This amazing Soviet sylph from the city of Grodno on the Neimen River near the Polish border actually represented the USSR military. The Ministry of Defense publicized her as a champion of the Soviet army.

During the pursuit of her education at Secondary School Number 10 in Grodno, Olga became a star pupil of the eccentric gymnastics instructor, Renald Ivanovoich Knysh. The innovative but demanding Knysh became Olga's mentor, instilling diligence and discipline into her life. So intimate was the teacher-pupil relationship that in a post-Olympics interview Korbut told a reporter that her victories in Munich were his as well as hers.

Prior to the 1972 Olympics, Olga, as a sixteen-year-old, won ovations from sympathetic Soviet audiences for her graceful acrobatics. She placed third in the all-round individual competition in the USSR National Gymnastic Championships at Kiev, and she later won that event in a major international meet at Riga, the capital city of Latvia.

In Munich, Olga, at seventeen years of age, was adopted by the fans from her very first appearance in the preliminary exercises. She wowed the crowds and charmed the world with her style and grace. She was the first gymnast to perform what is now known as a "flik-flak," a backward somersault on the uneven (asymmetrical) bars. Known for chancing risky and innovative routines, the fifty-seven-inch tall, eighty-eight-pound Soviet became known as the Munchkin of Munich.

Everything about Olga Korbut was tiny except her talent as a gymnast, and that was big enough to capture the hearts of millions. During the team competition, Olga's spectacular routine on the asymmetrical bars helped to vault the Soviets into gold-medal glory. Her performance solidified her place as the crowd favorite. Many ardent students of gymnastics thought she might have a chance of defeating the favored Lyudmila Tourischuva for the all-round championships.

On the day following Olga's sparkling performance in the team-combined exercises, she tasted the agony of defeat. On the asymmetrical bars where she had excelled twenty-four hours earlier, she stumbled, slipped off the bars, and missed a simple kip to remount. The judges gave her a 7.5, which resulted in a seventh-place finish for Olga in the all-round championship.[3]

The next day Olga came back with a vengeance and won two gold medals and one silver in the individual apparatus competition. She won a gold medal for the balance beam by scoring 19,400 points. That four-inch beam became to Olga a veritable platform, a stage, and made her a star.

Her score of 19,575 also merited her a gold medal in the floor exercises where it appeared that she had almost overcome gravity. In those exercises, one foot would touch the ground, and she would soar. The other foot would touch, and she would soar again. Her effort in this event was spellbinding. The silver medal was for her performance on the asymmetrical bars.

Even in the United States where Soviets were regarded with suspicion and antipathy, Olga's Olympic saga of triumph-failure-triumph won her the role of America's sweetheart. Her smile was the definition of innocence. Her tears expressed the pain of defeat that such innocence should never have to experience. She won not only America's heart, but she made the entire world fall in love.

She said, "I try to warm up before I go on. But the most important quality is a warm heart the audience knows."

It's that heart language that removes barriers and tears down walls.

If an eighty-eight-pound, fifty-nine-inch tall, seventeen-year-old gymnast managed to put a crack in the Iron Curtain, don't you think there is some kind of barrier you could remove, some kind of wall you could tear down, some kind of salve you could apply to a troubled world?

Everett Dirksen, an eloquent senator from Illinois, once said, "The oil can is mightier than the sword." The personality and performance of Olga Korbut in the Munich games was like oil, providing remedial relief to the hurts and the wounds of a strife-ridden world.

Christ who alone can provide ultimate peace has given to us the ministry of reconciliation (2 Cor. 5:18). Therefore, we must be busy tearing down the walls of hatred, resentment, strife, suspicion, fear, and prejudice. Furthermore, we must be engaged in building bridges of forgiveness, love, and acceptance.

A Gesture of Goodwill

Elana Meyer

The ominous cloud of racial segregation cast a dark shadow over America during my youth. African Americans, who were referred to by less complimentary names, were relegated to the back of the buses. Black Americans did not attend the public schools where I was enrolled. They had their own restrooms and water fountains, and they were often treated more like chattel than human beings.

Early in life I discovered that when bigotry invades the life of an individual, it strips him of all reason and logic. Tyrone Edwards said, "The prejudiced and obstinate man does not so much hold opinions, as his opinions hold him." I've seen many individuals trapped and held captive in the many prisons of prejudice. I have seen segregation choke the flow of God's blessings.

Through the years South Africa has operated under a system of racial segregation and white supremacy called apartheid. Ever since the first white settlement was founded in South Africa, racial segregation severely affected the social, cultural and economic structure of the nation. Not until the twentieth century, however, did racial segregation become an explicitly formulated program. Through apartheid, white supremacy was strengthened in the last half of the century until the election of F. W. DeKlerk as president of the republic in 1989. DeKlerk carefully and methodically took the necessary steps to end apartheid and establish the principle of equality among all the people of South Africa.

Although all apartheid laws have now been repealed and a new constitution has emerged, the real change must come in the hearts of the people. Sometimes a sincere and positive gesture of goodwill and acceptance is more powerful than all the legislation wise men can draft.

Enter Elana Meyer. Elana is perhaps the most notable personality on the African sports scene today. She is certainly the undisputed queen of South African athletics. Elana has set record times in several distances between 3,000 meters and 21.1 kilometers. She has been running for sixteen or seventeen years, and being white has given her the advantage of training at track-and-field facilities. Under apartheid, most blacks had little access to such specialized facilities.

Elana grew up with two sisters and a brother on a farm near Albertina in the Eastern Cape Province, not far from where the first Dutch and French Huguenot settlers stepped ashore in the seventeenth century. The farm on which she grew up had a rich family heritage and produced corn, wheat, ostriches, and sheep. Since Elana did not have the advantage of the kind of activities offered in a city, she used her own resources to entertain herself.

Running was her primary means of self-expression and entertainment. At the age of twelve she was sent to a boarding school where she began to run competitively. Under the guidance of an excellent coach, Elana scored significant victories in her track exploits. During this time she ran against Zola Budd, who became a major influence upon her career as a runner. She never really considered Zola an opponent but as a motivation to run faster.

Most Olympic enthusiasts remember Zola Budd as the runner who collided with American Mary Decker in the 3,000 meters in the 1984 games in Los Angeles. The incident provoked an international controversy and was an impediment to the careers of both runners.

In 1987 Elana graduated from the University of Stellenbosch with a bachelor's degree in communications, whereupon she was able to devote even more time to her training regimen. Elana began to mature as an athlete about the same time that South Africa began to mature as a nation. By 1990 Elana Meyer had begun to dominate her sport as Zola Budd once had. She set her sight on becoming a world-class runner.

In 1991 Meyer outran Budd in a major 3,000-meter showdown. Meyer also recorded the two fastest 5,000-meter times that year. By 1992 Elana was ready to represent South Africa in the Barcelona games. South Africa, with an integrated team, would be a participant again after a thirty-two-year absence. Meyer had been portrayed as a generally progressive, but nonpartisan citizen of a nation with a history of prejudice and unrest.

The eyes of the nations were upon her as she began the 10,000 meters. All the runners were bunched together during the first part of the race. Then Derartu Tulu of Ethiopia and Meyer broke away from the pack. The fact that Tulu won and Meyer placed second seemed to be of little significance. Tulu bested Meyer's time 31:06.02 to 31:11.75.[1] What happened after the crossing of the finish line was remarkably momentous: Elana and Derartu ran the emotional victory lap arm in arm. It was an incredible picture of unity and peace as the white Meyer and black Tulu demonstrated to the world the essence of the Olympic spirit.[2]

Perhaps as well as any Olympian, Elana knows that "there is neither Jew nor Greek, there is neither bond nor free, there is neither male nor female: for ye [we] are all one in Christ Jesus" (Gal. 3:28).

Elana is a Christian and unashamedly proclaims her faith. She unhesitatingly declares, "being a Christian involves having a personal, day-to-day relationship with God. . . . I am in the first place a Christian who happens also to be an athlete. The two are inseparable, you cannot say you are a Christian on Sundays when you go to church and when you have devotional times, but when you are training you are on your own.

"One can't take a degree, a car, nice clothing, track shoes, or anything else with one to heaven. One can only take people. So surely I must tell people about the Lord."[3]

Elana Meyer demonstrated the art of bridge building. Those who have the spirit of Christ will forestall favoritism, scorn segregation, pommel prejudice, and banish bigotry. Not only will the true Christian welcome all people to his fountain of water, but he will take them cups of cold water in Jesus' name. If he has only one cup, he will share, inviting his brother or sister to drink from the cup first.

The Ebony Antelope
Jesse Owens

Never has home-field advantage meant more than in the 1936 Olympic Games when athletes from around the world converged on Germany to compete on Adolph Hitler's turf. The advantage was decidedly in favor of the home team. The extreme nationalism that Hitler inspired, the careful development of world-class athletes, and a multitude of other things tipped the scales in favor of the host country.

By the time Berlin hosted the Eleventh Olympiad the Nazi juggernaut had gained considerable momentum. In 1925 there were 27,000 people in the Nazi Party in Germany. As the German democracy faltered, however, the Nazi Party grew in strength. By 1929 there were 176,000 in the party. Two years later there were 806,000, and by 1931 the party had almost 2 million devotees. On January 30, 1933,

Hitler was chosen as the chancellor of Germany and given dictatorial powers.[1]

A military machine with incredible war-making power was being developed under Hitler's watchful eye. The purpose of the military was to facilitate a new order for the nation based on Aryan supremacy. The so-called Aryans consisted of a segment of the Nordic race characterized by strength, beauty, and intelligence. To fulfill their self-appointed role as custodians of human culture, they determined that all of the *Untermenschen* ("subhumans") had to be eliminated. Therefore, the Reichsführer SS organized the systematic removal of more than 6 million Jews, gypsies, blacks, Slavs, communists, Catholics, and other human "animals." The methods of elimination included shooting, hanging, gassing, and burning.[2]

In a speech given to SS leaders, Heinrich Himmler, head of the Gestapo, said, "We must be honest, decent, loyal, and comradely to members of our own blood and to no one else. . . . Whether the other peoples live in comfort or die of hunger interests me only insofar as we need them as slaves."[3]

When Germany sponsored the 1936 Olympic Games in Berlin, Hitler seized it as an opportunity to showcase the remarkable progress and technological advances the nation had made under his leadership. The Führer had also developed programs designed to enhance and perfect the skills of the nation's athletes in preparation for the Berlin games. He desperately wanted the Olympics to validate his belief in the superiority of the Aryan race. He fully anticipated Germany's domination in every event.

Hitler was a powerful, persuasive, ruthless dictator. He wanted to dominate the world and was willing to use any means—noble or brutish—to accomplish his goal. He felt the same way about winning the Olympics. He once said,

"We have no scruples. . . . We are barbarians. We want to be barbarians. It is an honorable title."[4]

When the U.S. Olympic team arrived on the SS *Manhattan* at the port city of Bremerhaven, Germany, on June 24, 1936, they immediately saw the "new" Germany. Red, black, and white Nazi swastika flags were flying from every shop and street corner. The athletes traveled to Berlin on a contemporary and comfortable express train that afforded them an opportunity to see the well-groomed, verdant countryside. They also observed the broad and straight superhighways, called *autobahns.* The skies of Nazi Germany were dominated by huge hydrogen-filled airships called zeppelins. Taking things one step further, the Germans set a precedent for future games by constructing a beautiful and elaborate village specifically for the athletes from the visiting countries.[5]

The city of Berlin glittered with sparkling new structures and freshly painted buildings renovated for the games. The Olympic stadium was a cavernous arena with a capacity for 100,000 spectators. The Germans were fully prepared to impress the largest number of athletes—4,066—ever to participate in an Olympiad, host the most countries (49) ever to be represented, and entertain the most spectators ever assembled for the international games. Not even the worst enemy of the Nazi dictatorship could deny that the organizing committee had done a superlative job. Nonetheless, the general atmosphere surrounding the games provoked a sense of uneasiness and apprehension.

It was into this uncertain atmosphere that Jesse Owens and the U.S. Olympic team entered the 1936 games. Of course, Owens was no stranger to uncertainty and foreboding circumstances. He had been born James Cleveland Owens (nicknamed J. C.) on September 12, 1913, the tenth son of an Alabama sharecropper and the grandson of slaves. He joined his brothers and sisters in the grueling task of cultivating the fields, harvesting vegetables, and picking cotton. He was never very healthy as a child. Due to inadequate living conditions and a poor diet, he suffered chronic bronchial congestion that turned into pneumonia on several occasions.[6]

His physical problems included the appearance of strange boils on his chest and legs. Since there was no money for medicine or physicians, J. C.'s mother removed the terrifying growths surgically with the aid of a red-hot kitchen knife. Once J. C. stepped on a steel hunting trap, and on another occasion he was run over by a cotton wagon. That he managed to even survive his childhood is quite remarkable.[7]

In addition to his physical scars, he bore the psychological scars that came with a black sharecropper's family in Alabama. The poverty, the lack of adequate clothing, the lack of necessities, the suppression of blacks, all of these had a devastating and debilitating affect on J. C. as a lad.[8]

When J. C. was nine years old, the Owens family moved to Cleveland, Ohio, in search of a better life. They found an apartment in a ghetto neighborhood, and the family all went to work and pooled their wages to buy some of the luxuries they had only dreamed of possessing when they were in Alabama.[9]

J. C. was enrolled in Bolton Elementary School in Cleveland, and on the first day the teacher asked his name. "J. C.," he replied. Confused by his southern drawl, the teacher thought he had said Jesse, and the lad had a new name.[10]

Even as a boy Jesse loved to run. Running was something that he discovered that he could do alone. He could determine the distance, the direction, the pace, and the place for his running. In time he became a lithe, lean sprinter. He ran with fluid grace and was referred to as the "ebony antelope." His considerable accomplishments came without starting blocks and over tracks that would not be approved by modern standards.

In 1930 Jesse enrolled at the East Technical High School in Cleveland and won the admiration of his colleagues with his winsome smile and gregarious personality. At ETHS, Coach Charles Riley came into Jesse's life. Coach Riley became the powerful father figure Jesse never had and provided the encouragement and motivation he needed to begin to reach his potential. By Owens' junior year, he was so dominant in track-and-field competition that one newspaper referred to him as a one-man team.[11]

In the summer of 1932 Jesse went to Northwestern University to tryout for the U.S. Olympic team. He failed to qualify by losing out to Ralph Metcalf, who went on to the Los Angeles games where he won both a silver and bronze medal in the 100 meters and the 200 meters. Owens was not discouraged but felt that he had gained valuable experience in the tryout competition.[12]

Jesse returned to East Technical as a senior in the fall of 1932 and was elected president of the student body and captain of the track squad. Throughout the track season he thrilled his growing number of admirers by rolling up an unspoiled succession of victories for his team.[13]

In 1933 Jesse entered Ohio State University. He worked his way through college as a freight elevator operator. Even though he was extremely busy, he devoted a significant amount of time each day to training for the track season. In January 1934, Jesse was named to the American Athletic Union All-American Track Team. The remarkable thing about this prestigious honor is that it occurred before Jesse had competed in any collegiate track or field events.[14]

In 1935 Owens wrenched his back and jeopardized his chances of participating in the Big Ten championship meet. He looked more like a candidate for a convalescent home than a sporting event. He had to be helped from his car to the track. He even needed assistance in removing his warm-up outfit.

He dared not engage in any preliminary calisthenic exercises or running activities for fear of further injury. Surprisingly, during a forty-five-minute span that afternoon, Jesse Owens established five world records and tied a sixth. He equaled the world record for the 100-yard dash (9.4 seconds), set a world record for the broad jump (26 feet 18.25 inches), and set a world record for the 220 (20.3 seconds), which also broke the world record for the 200 meters. Additionally, he set a world's record for the 220-yard low hurdles (22.6 seconds). Jesse's heroic efforts that afternoon marked that day as perhaps the most significant day in the history of track-and-field competition.[15]

In 1936 the stage was set in Berlin for the Olympic Games. Hitler occupied his position of honor in the stadium, eager to watch his Aryans validate his racist philosophy. The opening ceremonies were completed with pomp and splendor. It was time for the games to begin.

No German athlete had ever won a gold medal in track-and-field competition. The stadium was filled to capacity. Every eye was riveted on the field for the first event of the day: the shot put. Hans Woellke, a German athlete, broke the Olympic record on his second effort in the shot put, and the predominantly German audience erupted with thunderous applause and shouted "heil" with considerable enthusiasm. Not only did Woellke win the first event in the 1936 games, but a fellow countryman, Gerhard Stoeck, won the bronze medal by finishing third.

Hitler must have felt smug, self-assured, elated, and confident as he sat in the loge of honor, savoring the victory. Woellke and Stoeck were escorted to the Führer's box, and the crowd expressed their approval as Hitler added his commendation to the victorious athletes. The 1936 games were developing just as the Nazi leader had planned and predicted.

Hitler soon discovered that Jesse Owens would be a fly in this ointment. While the Nazi dictator disdained what he considered inferior races, Owens had already begun to capture the hearts of the German people, especially the youth. Jesse's appealing personality and down-to-earth sense of humor made him a crowd favorite. He signed autographs, mingled with the people, and flashed a disarming smile, and the German people fell in love with him.[16]

When Owens broke the tape at 10.3 seconds in the 100-meter finals to break an Olympic record, the crowd honored him with a convulsive shout of congratulations and approval. Hitler did not share the delight of the amassed thousands. When Owens bowed to him from the victory platform, Hitler responded with a pained, stiff salute. The racial hatred that the Nazi leader had been trying to inspire for almost a decade was negated in ten seconds by a black man who had established a love relationship with the Olympic spectators.[17]

When an aide suggested that Hitler should invite Owens to the loge of honor, Hitler vehemently replied, "Do you really think that I will allow myself to be photographed shaking hands with a Negro?"[18]

Later Owens said of the Führer's snub, "It was all right with me. I didn't go to Berlin to shake hands with him anyway."[19]

In the Berlin games, Owens went on to win four gold medals. He broke two Olympic records, tied a third, and had a hand in a world-record relay. As Jesse bent forward to receive his gold medals and as he heard the national anthem, he knew he had achieved his dream. In succeeding years the gold of the medals that he had won in Berlin continued to shine even brighter and served to remind him of those days when his joy was greatest and his life the most fulfilled.

When Owens returned to the United States, job opportunities were limited, and he became a playground caretaker. The glory of the Olympics soon faded into the grind of a menial task. Distraught with his vocational lot in life, Jesse began to call upon his entrepreneurial spirit to find other ways to generate income.

In those years following the 1936 Olympics, Jesse landed a contract to lead a twelve-piece black touring band. Later he organized the Cleveland Olympians, a team of hotshots like the Harlem Globetrotters, to travel the country exhibiting their considerable basketball skills. Owens also organized a barnstorming softball team in the hope of paying off his debts. As a novelty act, he raced horses and motorcycles to establish some financial independence. Furthermore, he started a dry-cleaning business that failed in less than a year. Jesse even tried his hand at baseball, signing with a touring team known as the Indianapolis Clowns.[20]

Other work included government appointments as secretary of the Illinois State Athletic Commission and the executive directorship of a juvenile delinquency prevention program. During World War II, he accepted a job with the Civilian Defense Office and later became a personnel officer for the Ford Motor Company. Additionally, he worked in public relations and as an overseas goodwill representative of the government.

He finally made his mark as a public speaker. His winsome personality and his old-fashioned oratory was spellbinding. His diverse jobs and his demand as a public speaker took him from city to city. The typically indefatigable Owens began to weary of the incredible pace that he had maintained for years.[21]

Jesse awakened one day to the realization that he hardly knew his family. His three daughters had grown up in his absence, had left home, and were in pursuit of their own dreams. His wife, Ruth, had kept the home fires burning in an effort to provide a good family life for the Owens family. Jesse's barnstorming days and his constant travel had taken its toll. He realized that, to his own loss, he had neglected his wife and daughters.

Tony Gentry, in his biography of Jesse Owens, wrote, "Like the constant world traveler that he had become, Owens realized that his family existed for him primarily as snapshots in his wallet. Yet he could not stop himself. The constant running had begun to seem like a treadmill that he could not get off."[22]

In 1950 the Associated Press named Jesse Owens the greatest track-and-field athlete in history.[23] His life is an example of desire, drive, and determination. His charming personality and gregarious manner captured the hearts of millions. His successes are remarkable. His showdown with Hitler is the stuff sports legends are made of. But I wonder. I wonder about those gold medals that once hung around his neck. I wonder about those snapshots that he had in his wallet. I wonder what really meant the most—that which was represented by the medals or that which was represented by the snapshots.

A wise man once said, "they made me the keeper of the vineyards; but mine own vineyard have I not kept" (Song of Sol. 1:6). Sometimes we have the tendency to serve on committees and boards, take on additional projects, and give ourselves to more and more worthwhile humanitarian causes to the detriment of our own family. Look in your wallet. Is that snapshot all you have of your family?

That precious infant that you first saw in the delivery room quickly became a tiny toddler, seeking to climb into your lap. With time seemingly on fast forward, that little lad will be going to kindergarten and then first grade. Before you have a chance to get your breath, your elementary school student will become a Little Leaguer. The middle high school years will pass like a blur. Before you can tear the pages off your calendar, it seems you are taking a picture of him and his girlfriend as they make their way to the senior prom. Then when you write the check for that first college tuition payment, you wonder, *Where has the time gone?* All you have are a few memories, depending upon how much time you spent with your child, and the snapshot taken on the night of the prom.

Give your spouse and children the legacy of rich and rewarding experiences shared together. The investment of time in the life of your family members will reap incalculable dividends.

All That Glitters Is Not Gold

Dave Johnson

Few leading men in Hollywood are as strikingly handsome as Dave Johnson, the decathlete. His muscular physique tips the scales at two hundred pounds and is encased in an impressive six-foot-three-inch frame. He is a world-class athlete whose gutsy performance in the 1992 Olympic Games in Barcelona earned him the admiration of millions and a priceless, glittering medal.

If Johnson personified faith, courage, and determination in Barcelona, he embodied just the opposite of that while growing up in Montana, the big sky country. If eastern Montana is known for its "amber waves of grain," western Montana is known for its "purple mountain majesties." This picturesque part of the Rocky Mountains is so exquisitely beautiful that you'd be tempted to think God gave special attention to this part of His creative handiwork. This is where Dave Johnson was born and raised—scenic western Montana. Missoula to be exact.

Yet in the midst of this picturesque setting where the firmament obviously shows God's creative genius, Dave was a youth out of touch with his Creator. He was on a collision course with disaster. As a teenager, Dave's brushes with the law were many, but he prided himself on being faster than the police and knowing where to hide.

Mark Twain's philosophy about youth indicated that he knew some Dave Johnsons in his day. Twain said, "When a kid turns thirteen, stick him in a barrel, nail the lid shut and feed him through the knot hole. When he turns sixteen, plug the hole."[1] By the time Dave was sixteen years old, it seemed that he had thrown all restraint to the wind and was living a life of rebellion.

In 1982 God intervened in the apparent downward spiral in Dave's life by providing a job opportunity for his dad in Corvallis, Oregon. Dave found himself in a strange new environment just prior to his senior year in high school. The new locale obviously afforded him the opportunity to write a brand-new chapter in his life's book.

One of the first decisions Dave made upon arriving in Corvallis was to tryout for football at Crescent Valley High School. He reasoned that if he made the team he would be given instant visibility at the school. He knew that being on the team would help him bond with some of the most popular guys on campus. He also knew that football players were generally popular with girls.

To impress the coach, Dave identified himself as a wide receiver and discovered in the practice sessions that he was fast—the second fastest player on the team—and had the hand-eye coordination necessary to be an excellent receiver. His natural athletic ability surfaced almost immediately, and he made the team easily.

There was another wide receiver on the high school team by the name of Matt Hirte. Dave saw a dimension to Matt's life that set him apart from the other players on the team. While many of the football players chose to carouse and overindulge, Matt invested a good portion of his time in trying to develop a relationship with Dave. Matt spoke freely of the personal relationship he had with Jesus Christ. He indicated that Jesus had given to him a real sense of purpose and peace.

At first Dave tried to deflect Matt's Christian witness, but at the same time he admired his tenacity and persistence. There was a radiance about Matt's life that stood out like a diamond in a coal mine. As Dave continued to observe Matt's life, he realized that he not only admired him for his convictions, but that he was beginning to envy the kind of joy and contentment that Matt always seemed to possess, even when he spoke of heaven and hell. He knew that he had some major issues in his life that were unresolved.

Dave started thinking about his past—his rebellion against his parents, the people he had hurt, the mistakes he had made, the dismal record of his years in Missoula, the realization that he had stayed out of jail, not because of his moral rectitude, but because of his imaginative elusiveness. Dave also started thinking about his future. He had no dreams, no goals, no ambitions, no plans after high school.

Matt's personal faith and purpose-driven life began to make more sense to Dave than his own aimless existence. He asked to borrow Matt's Bible to explore some of the truths that his teammate had shared with him. Dave read the Gospel of John, then Matthew, Mark, and Luke and decided that it was time to surrender his life to God.

Dave prayed to receive Jesus Christ as his personal savior. Immediately the gray ghost of guilt that had been haunting him was gone. The burden of his past sins was lifted, and Dave Johnson was born again. He knew that his heart was clean at last, and he was ready to live for Christ.[2]

After graduating from high school, Dave went to Western Oregon State College in Monmouth. His failure to get into a church or a Bible study, and the absence of his friend, Matt, to provide accountability, proved that Dave needed structure—someone or something to fan the flame that had been ignited when he gave his life to Christ.

That structure and nurturing finally came when Dave transferred to Azusa Pacific University in Southern California. In this Christian college, Dave found the family of faith he needed to encourage him to be a strong and consistent Christian. At APU, Dave met Terry Franson, the track coach who became his spiritual mentor. Coach Franson was able to instill in Dave's heart the importance of living to glorify God. Under the influence of his new mentor, Dave was destined to develop into a world-class decathlete and to use the sports arena as his platform for serving the Lord.

Early in his tenure at APU, Dave established two ambitious goals for himself: to compete in the 1984 Olympic trials and to score 8,000 points in a decathlon meet. The goals were fairly grandiose and perhaps even unreasonable for a decathlete with such limited experience. To the astonishment of almost everyone, however, both goals were realized, and Dave was on his way to becoming a world-class decathlete.

Two years later Dave won the first of his four national championships. In early 1992 a determined Dave scored 8,727 points in a decathlon, only 120 points under the world record. He appeared to be primed and ready for the Olympic Games in Barcelona.

Reebok Corporation launched a $25 million ad campaign promoting the rivalry between Dave Johnson and fellow U.S. decathlete Dan O'Brien. According to the promotional hype, each man viewed himself as the world's greatest athlete, a distinction that would finally be determined at the Barcelona games.[3]

Dave and Dan became household names. Billboards everywhere portrayed their rivalry. Commercials heralded the competition between the two superathletes. For more than two years the rival U.S. decathlete stars battled to see who would emerge as the world's greatest athlete.

At the Olympic trials in New Orleans, Dan O'Brien was on a world-record pace in the decathlon when it came time for the pole vault. Surprisingly, he was eliminated from the Barcelona games because he failed in the pole vault. Additionally, Christian Schenk, the seven-foot-six-inch defending gold medalist, failed to make his team in the Olympic trials in Germany. Although he was leading through eight events in the Olympic trials and headed for his best score ever, he took a cortisone shot for a sore elbow that resulted in a bizarre no-score in the javelin. Schenk's hand was numbed due to the injection, and he couldn't hold the javelin. His desperate attempts to register some kind of a score were futile, and he was disqualified from Olympic competition.

Dave was beginning to look like the strong favorite to win in the Olympic Games in Spain. Yet, before those Olympic trials, Dave began to feel a sharp, unpredictable pain in his right foot. He had developed a stress fracture in the navicular bone in his right foot. Even though he experienced intense pain, Dave ran hard, performed well, took first place at the trials, and broke the Olympic record.

Dave's success at the trials did not come without a cost, however. An MRI (magnetic resonance imaging) revealed a major crack in the navicular bone in his right foot. Dave stood on the threshold of winning a gold medal in the

Olympic Games, but that bone fracture had the potential of reducing his greatest goal to a foolish dream.

Although Dave had trained six hours a day for ten years to be at his best for the 1992 games, he knew that this fracture introduced a huge negative factor. Yet he felt that this was a time when his faith would help him overcome this enormous physical impediment. He wanted the people of America, especially young people, to see him as a competitor and not as a quitter.

In Barcelona the first five events in the decathlon were scheduled for August 5. Hoping to give his stress fracture some time to heal, Dave had not worked out in three and a half weeks. Nevertheless, these were his days of destiny, and he was prepared to give 100 percent to each of the ten events so he might glorify God at the Twenty-fifth Olympiad.

In the first event, the 100 meters, Dave sprinted out of the blocks with splendid acceleration. Because he had not trained in almost a month, his legs felt rubbery after 50 meters, and he struggled to finish at 11.6 seconds. The time was adequate, but not what he had hoped to accomplish. Almost immediately, he felt a new, acute pain, but trusted God to sustain him.

The second event was the long jump, and Dave managed to generate enough speed to jump 24.1 feet, even though his personal best was almost 25 feet. He lost a few points. His participation in the event, however, did not seem to tax the stress fracture because he didn't have to jump off the injured foot and he ended his leap in the sand, which provided something of a cushion for his landing.

The third event in the decathlon is the shot put, and all Dave's weight, plus the 16-pound shot put, was pressing down on the right foot. This event begins by balancing all your weight on the right foot and ends up the same way. At this point the pain was intensifying, and Dave was not adjusting well to the kind of spinning and turning necessary to throw this 16-pound iron ball.

The official called a foul on Dave in each of his three attempts. Had the decision stood, Dave would have fouled out and been disqualified for further competition in the decathlon. Another official overruled the first judge and awarded Dave a fourth attempt. The U.S. decathlete accepted this additional chance as a gift from God, overcame the hisses and boos of the biased, predominantly Spanish spectators, and threw the shot put for a personal record and set the pace for the two final events of the day.

The fourth event was the high jump, which Dave made at six feet seven inches. He had hoped to exceed his personal best of six feet eleven inches, but he felt an increasing pain as he turned to catapult himself over the bar. Even though Dave demonstrated a valiant effort, major points were lost again.

The final event of the day was the 400 meters, the very event in which Dave had injured his foot in practice almost a month earlier. Through sheer determination he ran the first half of the race faster than he had ever run it, but the lack of training once again took its toll, and he didn't have the strength to finish at that kind of pace. He finished with a time of 49.7 seconds, a phenomenal achievement for a man with a broken ankle; however, Dave was hoping to run the race in 47.8 seconds. He was discouraged and began to feel the gold medal slipping away.

By the end of the day a cadre of reporters and cameramen surrounded Dave. Questions were fired in rapid succession. Even though he had not so much as hinted at a problem, they sensed that something was wrong. He wanted his injury to be a private faith experience and didn't want to make any excuses, for he did not believe that

Christ would make excuses if He were competing in the decathlon.

The next day, August 6, 1992, the first event was the high hurdles—an event that was destined to push the limit of Dave's pain threshold and likely exacerbate the injury. In this event an athlete goes over ten hurdles at top speed. Dave's right leg was his lead leg, which meant that ten times in this event he would descend with all of his weight on the injured foot and ankle. Midway through the race, as he came down on the injured foot, Dave heard a popping sound in his ankle and felt a wave of pain radiate to every part of his body. Later he discovered that the navicular bone splintered in another direction, and the problem had increased appreciably. He finished the race with a time of 14.8 seconds and lost yet more points.

Dave's discouragement was beginning to turn to considerable apprehension over the potential physical consequences of continuing his quest for an Olympic medal. Coach Terry Franson, friends, and family members urged him to press on. Driven by his faith and commitment, he decided to continue one event at a time.

The seventh of the ten events was the discus, "the metal Frisbee" as Dave calls it. In this event he challenged his personal best record of 168 feet by throwing the 4-pound-6.5-ounce Frisbee almost 160 feet. He lost a few points, but his total points were continuing to climb.

The eighth event was the pole vault. After arching over the bar at 16 feet 8 inches, Dave opted not to try to better the mark. It was a matter of wisdom not to risk further damage, because the stress fractures were experiencing some trauma and affecting the rest of the ankle as well. The swelling was profound, and the pain excruciating.

The next-to-last event was the javelin—Dave's best

event and one for which he held the American record. He felt confident that he could succeed under any circumstance but soon realized that he did not have the flexibility in his right foot to turn and throw the javelin according to his customary style. He ended up throwing this Olympic spear from a standing position and managed to take second place in this event, even though his Barcelona effort was 45 to 50 feet less than his average throw.

The final decathlon event was the 1,500 meters. Francis "Daley" Thompson of Great Britain, who won the gold medal in the decathlon at the 1980 and 1984 games, said, "The decathlon is nine Mickey Mouse events and a 1,500 M." So now Dave was faced with having to run a mile on a fractured, distressed, and traumatized ankle.

The coaches were continuing to challenge Dave to complete his mission. They reminded him that, remarkably, he still had a chance to win the bronze medal. Dave received some considerable relief for the pain in his foot with a shot of Novocaine. He prayed, "Lord, help me get through these 1,500 meters. Help me to do what You've always taught me to do—to give 100 percent. And help me do it to glorify Your name."

Having prayed that prayer, Dave stepped on the track for the final event. The tension was incredible, the fear intense, the foot numb, but the faith of Dave Johnson was still strong. He knew the Lord was in control of the situation and that from his experience in Barcelona there would be a story to tell that would somehow honor the Lord.

In the 1,500 meters Dave managed to stay ahead of those who might have been able to wrest the bronze medal from him. He finished the decathlon in third place, realizing that God's will had been accomplished. Had he won the gold medal and broken the Olympic record, as many thought he would, his story would not have been nearly so dramatic. It would have been perhaps too perfect.

Dave says, "God has called me to talk about a bronze medal and a broken bone. Kids need to know that there are obstacles to overcome—that they must have faith in God to succeed. Give yourself 100 percent to God, and although you may not all win gold medals, there will be gold in your hearts."[4]

Dave Johnson is a world-class athlete winning at life. He has not won the gold medal—yet—but his bronze medal shines with an incredible brightness. In truth, all that glitters is not gold.

I have always admired those who are willing to play through pain, to continue to play though they were hurting. The apostle Paul did that. He had some kind of terrible affliction, and he prayed three times that God would remove it. Yet God chose to give Paul grit and grace instead of good health.

What was Paul's response? He said, "Most gladly therefore will I rather glory in my infirmities, that the power of Christ may rest upon me. Therefore I take pleasure in infirmities, in reproaches, in necessities, in persecutions, in distresses for Christ's sake: for when I am weak, then am I strong" (2 Cor. 12:9b–10).

Paul was a physical wreck, but he didn't throw in the towel; he didn't quit. He continued to do what God had called him to do. Furthermore, he did it with greater effectiveness and with greater power than ever before. Paul's refusal to quit, though wracked with pain, resulted in greater glory for God than would have been possible otherwise.

Yield your life to God. Allow Him to translate your brokenness into a blessing. In fact, if you are weak and powerless, you may be the very person that God is looking for to prove Himself strong in the eyes of a skeptical and disbelieving world. It may be the bronze of your life that God will use to outshine all the fool's gold this world has to offer.

Cool under Pressure
Mary Lou Retton

Nadia Comaneci of Rumania attracted the attention of millions when she won the all-round gold medal for women's gymnastics at the 1976 Olympic Games in Montreal. Among those millions, however, she specifically attracted the attention of eight-year-old Mary Lou, the daughter of Ron Retton, who had played basketball with Jerry West at the University of West Virginia and later was a shortstop in the New York Yankees farm system.

Mary Lou was stretched out on the floor of the family room in her Fairmont, West Virginia, home, watching Nadia perform her routines. As a beginner in gymnastics, Mary Lou was enthralled and challenged by the precision of Comaneci's acrobatics, but at that time she could not possibly have known that one day she would be the heir to the gymnastic throne.

With the passing of time, Mary Lou began to demonstrate remarkable ability in her gymnastic training and began to dream of the Olympics. When Bela Karolyi, who had trained Comaneci in Rumania, defected to the United States in 1981, the pixie from Fairmont placed herself under his tutelage.

Mary Lou willingly submitted to the stringent discipline outlined by Karolyi. She gave up her childhood. She missed proms, ball games, and school events. She devoted herself to gymnastics. Karolyi pounded and molded her into a world-class gymnast. She had developed into a four-foot-nine-inch, ninety-two-pound package of power and personality plus. As she amassed one victory after another, she began to radiate confidence. Her sparkling smile won the hearts of audiences wherever she performed.

She had set her sights on the Olympic Games in Los Angeles in 1984. But less than six weeks before the midsummer spectacular was to begin, Mary Lou developed a gimpy knee. Her doctors told her to forget about the upcoming Olympiad and to wait until 1988. She decided to take her chances with orthoscopic surgery and flew to Richmond, Virginia, where torn cartilage in her right knee was successfully repaired. She was back in the gym the next day. She worked out on a bicycle—pedaling, pushing, driving herself. Within a week she was expanding her scope of exercises to the amazement of all. Through sheer grit and determination she readied herself for the ultimate competition of the Olympic Games.

The odds were definitely not in her favor. No American woman had ever won an individual Olympic gymnastics medal of any kind. Although Mary Lou had been enjoying great success in her rounds of competition, she had precious little international experience. When she arrived in Los Angeles, she realized that her chief opponents were three Rumanians who had come to California to claim the medals—all the medals. Ectarina Szabo, a relentless deadpan blonde of seventeen, was Rumania's national champion and the European junior champion of 1980 and 1982. She had collected five perfect scores in a world meet in Budapest in 1983.

The match-up in Los Angeles' Pauley Pavilion began to look something like the duel at the OK Corral, only on a larger scale. Retton, along with her U.S. counterparts—Kathy Johnson and Julianne McNamara—entered the arena wearing American-flag leotards that displayed stripes here and stars there. The fan-atics, 9,023 of them, had already been whipped into a frenzy over this event through media hype.[1]

The event began with Mary Lou leading all thirty-six women with a score of 39.525 points, which were carried over from her performance in the team competition. Szabo was only .15 points behind with an initial 39.375 total.

Szabo began her evening's work with a stunning performance on the balance beam that earned her a perfect score of 10. Her routine included four consecutive back walkovers, each finished with perfectly balanced landings on the four-inch-wide beam. The superbly graceful performance earned her perfect scores from all four judges.

Meanwhile, the best Mary Lou could do on the uneven bars was an unsteady 9.85. Szabo and Retton were now tied at 49.375.

The second rotation took Szabo to the floor exercises and Retton to the balance beam. During the floor routine, the romping Rumanian displayed brilliant control of her compact body. Perhaps in an effort to psych out her U.S. rival, Szabo selected "The Battle Hymn of the Republic" rather than the traditional classical music to guide her through her up-tempo paces. She went through her routine magnificently, with only the slightest flaw, and was awarded a 9.95.

On the beam Mary Lou had two shaky landings. Her double-somersaulting dismount won the overwhelming approval of the audience but only a 9.80 score from the judges. Retton trailed Szabo by .15.

After her vaulting earned her a solid score of 9.90, Szabo had an opportunity to watch Retton's floor exercises, which she did to distinctly Eastern European–style music. Mary Lou's dazzling routine could not have helped Ectarina's confidence. America's newest sweetheart soared to phenomenal heights, appearing as if she was launching her stunts from a trampoline. She performed routines beyond the reach of all other women gymnasts. She was awarded a perfect score and now trailed Szabo by only .05 points. The stage was set for the final routine.

Szabo had scored nothing less than a 9.9 during the evening's routines, which was also her score on the final event, the uneven parallel bars. As Mary Lou paced the runway, awaiting her time on the vault, she watched Ectarina's performance out of the corner of her eye. She saw her opponent take a little step on her dismount and concluded that that one tiny error would cost her. Indeed, Szabo was given another 9.9; 9.95 would have given her a share of the gold and 10.0 would have given her the championship of the all-round event. Szabo's slight misstep created an opportunity for Mary Lou. Now Karolyi's student had the moment she wanted.

Mary Lou turned toward her coach and with an undaunted smile said, "I'm going to stick it." In gymnastics that means finishing the routine with a perfect landing, upright and without a wobble. If Mary Lou could finish either of her vaults with such a perfect finish, she would win by .05 of a point—anything less and she would have the consolation of the silver medal.

As Retton squared her shoulders to face the vault at the end of the runway, the audience, realizing the significance of the moment, began to applaud insanely. The teenager from West Virginia hurled herself into flight on her powerful legs, sprinting, soaring, diving, and she finished perfectly. Had there been a script for this dramatic evening in Pauley Pavilion, Mary Lou performed as though she was the author. The biased audience shouted, "10—10—10." Moments later the judges revealed that they concurred and awarded a perfect score. Retton raised her arms in victory and smiled adoringly to the admiring crowd. Mary Lou had just inserted herself into Olympic history as the first American gymnast to win a gold medal.

Bela Karolyi credited Retton as a cinch to win because she was the most powerful gymnast ever to compete in the sport and because of her ability to excel under pressure. He declared, "She's got the psychological power to go through the moments when everyone else is falling apart."

By scoring back-to-back tens in her final routines, the new American folk heroine with the megawatt smile overcame pressure of Olympic proportions. Her feat was comparable to a major league pitcher hurling two shutouts in the World Series to help his team win the championship ring, or an NFL running back covering the distance of the field in his last two carries to win the Super Bowl.

Mary Lou went on to win four other medals (two silver and two bronze) in the 1984 games. The buoyant but unpretentious pixie wrapped her medals in a plastic bag and put them under her bed. Only recently did Shannon Kelly, Mary

Lou's husband and former Texas Longhorn quarterback, talk her into having them set in glass and hung on the wall of their Houston home.

Nine years after winning the gold medal in Los Angeles, Mary Lou stood in the Second Baptist Church of Houston, Texas, and radiated a profound love for Jesus Christ as she narrated a thrilling, God-blessed patriotic worship service. She declared, "Physical strength comes from training, lifting one more weight. Or in the case of a gymnast, doing one more flip. But real courage and real strength comes from God."[2]

Would you like to have the courage and strength to live life to its fullest? The Bible uses terminology derived from the ancient Olympic Games to challenge us and give us direction.

In Hebrews 12 one might well imagine a huge Olympic stadium filled to capacity. The runners are in the starting blocks, poised to begin the race. Suddenly they're off. The spectators cheer. The athletes strive for the mastery of their sport. The finish line is in sight. The tape is broken! The winner is honored with a medal of gold!

Hear the words of the ancient writer of truth: "Wherefore seeing we also are compassed about with so great a cloud of witnesses, let us lay aside every weight, and the sin which doth so easily beset us, and let us run with patience the race that is set before us, Looking unto Jesus the author and finisher of our faith; who for the joy that was set before him endured the cross, despising the shame, and is set down at the right hand of the throne of God" (Heb. 12:1–2).

1. The Race: The Bible compares life to a race. When you are born, you enter the race. For some it is little more than a rat race, but the race of life must be more than an endless round of circles, aimless dashes here and there.

God our Creator has placed us in this race, and He wants it to be a joyful, fulfilling experience. God loves us and wants us to have a sense of purpose in this marathon called life. Jesus, God's Son, said, "I am come that they might have life, and that they might have it more abundantly" (John 10:10). That means you! God wants you to have life to its fullest.

2. The Rules: Every race has rules and regulations. An infraction of the rules could result in a disqualification. As the race of life is run, every weight or sin must be eliminated. When Dave Johnson was running the 100 meters in the decathlon with a stress fracture in the navicular bone of his right ankle, he said, "It was like running with a bear on my back."

With all due respect to bears, when our lives are cluttered with sin, it is like running with a bear on our back. Sins have a crippling effect upon our lives, and we're all guilty. The Bible says, "For all have sinned, and come short of the glory of God" (Rom. 3:23), and, "The wages of sin is death" (Rom. 6:23).

3. The Remedy: Since we cannot successfully complete life's race burdened down with our sins, Jesus Christ has been offered to us as our sinbearer. The Bible says, "All we like sheep have gone astray; we have turned every one to his own way; and the LORD [God] hath layed on him [Jesus] the iniquity of us all" (Isa. 53:6).

God's answer to our sin problem is Jesus Christ: "For God so loved the world, that he gave his only begotten Son, that whosoever believeth in him should not perish, but have everlasting life" (John 3:16).

The choice is yours. You can know God's love when you accept Jesus into your life and choose to follow Him.

This is what Jesus is saying to you right now: "Behold, I stand at the door, and knock: if any man hear my voice, and open the door, I will come in to him, and will sup with him, and he with me" (Rev. 3:20).

Since Jesus Christ is knocking at your heart's door, invite Him to come into your life. Call upon the Lord by praying the following prayer of commitment.

> Dear Lord Jesus, I know that I am a sinner. I am sorry for my sins. I know that I cannot save myself. I believe that You died on the cross for me and rose from the grave that I might have everlasting life. Come into my heart. Forgive me of my sins. Give me a clean heart and a conscience that is free from guilt. Take control of my life and help me to be the person that You want me to be. Save me now and forever, in Jesus' name. Amen.

If you sincerely prayed that prayer, God has promised to save you and to give you eternal life. Romans 10:13 says, "For whosoever shall call upon the name of the Lord shall be saved."

4. The Result: The result of having Christ in your life is victory. Christ will put a spring in your step, a song in your heart, and significance in your life. He replaces guilt with peace, bondage with freedom, defilement with cleansing, sadness with joy, frustration with fulfillment, and meaninglessness with purpose and direction. As the apostle Paul said, "we are more than conquerors through him that loved us" (Rom. 8:37).

Like Mary Lou Retton, Dave Johnson, and countless other world-class athletes, you are on the winning team.

When Jesus is the most important thing in your life, you can't lose. He has promised you a meaningful, purposeful life that will last you all the way to the finish line and beyond.

NOTES

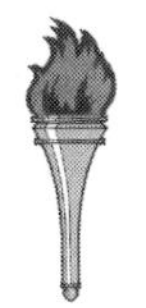

Chapter 1

1. Bill Henry and Patricia Henry Yeomans, *An Approved History of the Olympic Games* (Sherman Oaks, Calif.: Alfred Publishing Co., 1984), page prior to chapter one.
2. David Wallechinsky, *The Complete Book of the Olympics* (Boston: Little, Brown & Co., 1992), 93.
3. Ibid., 26.
4. Ibid., 33.
5. Ibid., 39.
6. Interview with Jim Mellado, director of the Willow Creek Association at Willow Creek, Barrington, Ill., May 19, 1995.
7. Wallechinsky, *The Olympics,* 91.
8. *Encyclopedia Americana,* 1964 ed., s.v. "Prometheus."
9. Ibid., s.v. "Statue of Liberty."
10. *World Book,* 1986 ed., s.v. "Olympic Games."
11. Henry and Yeomans, *Approved History,* 178.
12. Ibid., 228.
13. Ibid., 303.

14. Ibid., 330.
15. Ibid., 361.
16. Ibid., 395.
17. Patt Morrison and Andrew H. Malcolm, "All the Way Across the U.S.A.," *Reader's Digest,* November 1984, 150.
18. Ibid., 150–51.
19. Michael Finkel, "The Run of a Lifetime: Five Hundred Meters of Glory as a Carrier of the Olympic Torch," *Skiing,* October 1994, 42–43.
20. *Encyclopedia Americana,* 1964 ed., s.v. "Olympia."
21. James Coote, *The 1980 Book of the Olympics: The Games Since 1896—A Pictorial Record* (London, England: Exeter Books, 1980), 7.
22. Ibid., 8.

Chapter 2

1. James C. Hefley, *Sports Alive* (Grand Rapids, Mich.: Zondervan Publishing House, 1966), 74.
2. Wallechinsky, *The Olympics,* 606.

Chapter 3

1. Lisa H. Albertson, ed., "Tokyo—Against All Odds," in *Athens to Atlanta: 100 Years of Glory* (Salt Lake City, Utah: Commemorative Publications, 1993), 163.
2. Wallechinsky, *The Olympics,* 607.

Chapter 4

1. Wallechinsky, *The Olympics,* 21.
2. Ibid.
3. Ibid.
4. Gene Brown, ed., *The New York Times Encyclopedia of Sports: Track & Field,* vol. 4 (Danbury, Conn.: Arno Press, 1979), 39.
5. Lisa H. Albertson, ed., "Chariots of Reality," in *Athens to Atlanta,* 87.
6. Martin Connors, Diane L. Dupuis, and Brad Morgan, *The Olympics Factbook: A Spectator's Guide to the Winter and Summer Games* (Detroit, Mich.: Visible Ink Press, 1992), 517.
7. Albertson, "Chariots of Reality," 86.

Chapter 6

1. Wallechinsky, *The Olympics,* xxiii.

Chapter 8

1. Frank Deford, "A Track Full of Miracles," *Newsweek,* August 10, 1992, 29.
2. Clayton L. Thomas, ed., *Taber's Cyclopedic Medical Dictionary* (Philadelphia: F. A. Davis Co., 1985), 696.
3. Kenny Moore, "Dash to Glory," *Sports Illustrated,* August 10, 1992, 18.
4. Deford, "Track Full of Miracles," 29.

Chapter 9

1. Wallechinsky, *The Olympics,* 444.

Chapter 11

1. Wallechinsky, *The Olympics,* 37–38.
2. Franz Lidz, "They're All My Children," *Sports Illustrated,* December 21, 1987, 24–25.

Chapter 12

1. Kent R. Hill, *The Soviet Union on the Brink* (Portland, Oreg.: Multnomah, 1991), 18.
2. Leigh Montville, "Return of the Pixies," *Sports Illustrated,* November 27, 1989, 32–36.
3. Wallechinsky, *The Olympics,* 379.

Chapter 13

1. Lisa H. Albertson, ed., *Barcelona—Albertville 1992* (Colorado Springs: U.S. Olympic Committee, 1992), 65.
2. John Brant, "On the Right Track," *Runner's World,* July 1993.
3. Article on "Elana Meyer—On the Right Side of the Track."

Chapter 14

1. Richard Tames, *Nazi Germany* (London, England: Batsford Academic and Educational Co., 1985), 7.
2. Ibid., 17.
3. Ibid.
4. Ibid., 5.
5. Ibid., 60.
6. Tony Gentry, *Jesse Owens* (New York: Chelsea House Publishers, 1990), 19.
7. Ibid., 20.
8. Robert Helmick, *The Olympic Spirit: Portraits of Hope and Excellence* (Colorado Springs: U.S. Olympic Committee, 1992), 41–42.
9. Gentry, *Jesse Owens,* 24.
10. Ibid., 25.
11. Ibid., 32.
12. Ibid., 36.
13. Ibid., 37–38.
14. Ibid., 43.
15. Ibid., 45.
16. Ibid., 61.
17. Ibid., 64–65.
18. Ibid.
19. Jesse Owens, Champion of the Century, program from the 1995 Jesse Owens Award Banquet.
20. Gentry, *Jesse Owens,* 85–86.
21. Ibid., 91–96.
22. Ibid., 97–98.
23. Ibid., 95.

Chapter 15

1. James S. Hewett, ed., *Illustrations Unlimited* (Wheaton, Ill.: Tyndale House Publishers, 1988), 498.
2. Verne Becker, "The Spirit Behind Dave Johnson," *The New Man: For Men of Integrity,* September-October 1994, 21–24.
3. Sally B. Donnelly, "Dave on His Own," *Time,* July 27, 1992, 62–63.
4. Dave Johnson, interview with Bill Hybels, Willow Creek Community Church, 1993.

Chapter 16

1. Bob Ottum, "A Vault Without Fault," *Sports Illustrated,* August 13, 1984, 43.
2. Mary Lou Retton, "The Champion," *The Winning Walk* (videotape), Second Baptist Church, Houston, Texas.